Proceedings of a Japan Society for the Promotion of Science Seminar

TRENDS
IN
SUPERCOMPUTING

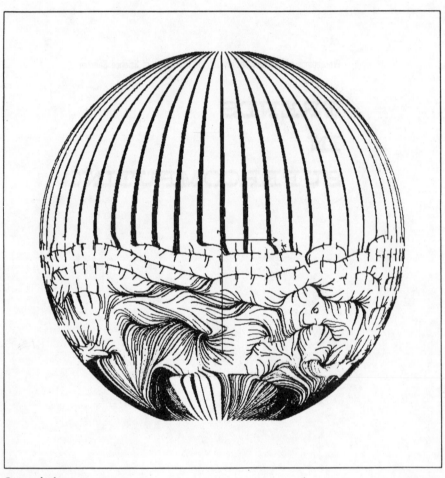

Cover design:

Flow around a sphere at Reynolds number 100000. Surface streamlines are shown. Initially laminar flow separates and becomes turbulent.

球をすぎる流れの表面流線。レイノルズ数100000。
始めに層流であった流れが剥離して乱流に遷移している。

Proceedings of a Japan Society for the Promotion of Science Seminar

TRENDS IN SUPERCOMPUTING

Editors

Y Kanada
Computer Centre
University of Tokyo

C K Yuen
Department of Information Systems
and Computer Science
National University of Singapore

World Scientific
Singapore • New Jersey • London • Hong Kong

Published by

World Scientific Publishing Co. Pte. Ltd.
P O Box 128, Farrer Road, Singapore 9128

USA office: World Scientific Publishing Co., Inc.
687 Hartwell Street, Teaneck, NJ 07666, USA

UK office: World Scientific Publishing Co. Pte. Ltd.
73 Lynton Mead, Totteridge, London N20 8DH, England

Library of Congress Cataloging-in-Publication Data

Trends in supercomputing.
Bibliography: p.
Includes index.
Proceedings of a seminar on supercomputing held at the Computer Centre
of the University of Tokyo, 1988, sponsored by the Japan Society for the
Promotion of Science.
1. Supercomputers—Congresses.   I. Kanada, Y.   II. Yuen, C. K.
III. Nihon Gakujutsu Shinkokai.
QA76.5.T69   1988   004.1'1   88-33807
ISBN 9971-50-831-1

Printed in Singapore by JBW Printers & Binders Pte. Ltd.

Preface

The present volume records the proceedings of a seminar
on the subject of Supercomputing, held at the Computer
Centre of the University of Tokyo (CCUT), over four
days in May-June 1988. The seminar was the seventh
seminar in the Japan-Singapore Academic Exchange
Programme sponsored by the Japan Society for the
Promotion of Science (JSPS). Under this Programme, some
260 academics have made exchange visits between the two
countries, and six earlier seminars on various
scientific themes have been held, either in Japan or in
Singapore.

A total of 56 persons attended the Supercomputing
seminar, 42 from Japan, 12 from Singapore, and 1 each
from USA and Canada. The JSPS provided generous
financial support for the seminar, in the form of
airfare and living expenses for 10 delegates from
Singapore, and all of the seminar running cost,
including the purchase of copies of the published
proceedings for the delegates. For this support we
express our deepest appreciations to JSPS. Local
organizational support was provided by the CCUT under
the direction of Professor E Goto, to whom much credit
must go for the smooth running and efficient effort.

In accordance with the normal seminar format, there
were a number of technical sessions in which papers
were presented by researchers from the two countries
describing their own work, on both the application of
supercomputers and the software and hardware technology
underlying the machines. These technical papers have
now been collected together into this published volume.

In addition, the delegates were able to tour the CCUT
supercomputer installation housing a Hitachi S-820
model 80; the Hitachi Kanagawa Manufacturing Facility,
where various supercomputer models are assembled; the
Institute for Computational Fluid Dynamics, Tokyo,
housing the NEC and Fujitsu machines used in computing
the simulation results described by Professor Kuwahara
in this volume; and the Information Processing Centre
and the Electro Technical Laboratory of the Agency of
Industrial Science and Technology at Tsukuba, housing a
recently installed Cray X-MP machine and the SIGMA-1
Dataflow Supercomputer now under development. There
were also product presentations from Fujitsu, NEC, ETA
and Cray.

The proceedings is divided into four parts. The five
papers of Part 1 describe the application of
supercomputer computation and simulation methods to
problems in various fields of science. The papers of

Part 2 discuss a number of mathematical applications.
Part 3 is concerned with language and compiler
optimization issues that arise from vector processing.
The three papers of Part 4 cover discussions of the
performance of current supercomputer systems and new
technology for configuring future supercomputer
systems.

We wish to thank all the authors for their time and
effort in preparing and presenting their papers. We
ourselves have found the seminar a very worthwhile and
highly instructive experience, and are pleased to be
able to share this, at least in part, with the reader,
who, I am sure, will want to join us in thanking the
many individuals and organizations that together helped
to make all this possible.

Y Kanada
C K Yuen
October 1988

TABLE OF CONTENTS

Preface v

Seminar Opening Address ix

Part 1
Supercomputer Application in the Natural Sciences

Flow Simulation on Supercomputer 3
    Kunio Kuwahara

Application of Super-Computers in Weather Prediction 10
    Lim Hock

An Introduction to Atmospheric General Circulation Model (Abstract) 19
    Tatsushi Tokioka

Satellite Remote Sensing Applications 21
    Y. J. Chong

A Supercomputer-Based Neural Network Simulating System 26
    K. F. Loe, L. S. Hsu, S. C. Chan & H. B. Low

Part 2
Supercomputer Application in Mathematics

Vectorization of Lewis-Payne Random Number Generation on
HITAC S810 and S820 47
    Yoshio Oyanagi

Large Scale Nonlinear Optimization Using a Cyber 205 Supercomputer 51
    K. H. Phua

Supercomputer Oriented Numerical Algorithms for Sparse
Matrix Computation 73
    Takashi Nodera

Calculation of pi to the 33 Million Decimal Places as Benchmark and
Heat Run Tests (Abstract)   88
    Yasumasa Kanada

Performance of Supercomputer Versions of NUMPAC (Abstract)   89
    Ichizo Ninomiya & Yasuyo Hatano

Part 3
Software Techniques for Supercomputing

VFP: Vectorized Interpreter of the Functional Programming Language FP   93
    M. Shimasaki, K. Hirai & T. Tsuda

Compiling Optimizations through Program Transformations   109
    Michiaki Yasumura

Part 4
Hardware Technology for Supercomputing

Quantum Flux Parametron and Neural Network Modelling   163
    E. Goto & K. F. Loe

A Proposed Generalization of the Topology of the
Connection Machine   172
    M. C. Lee, C. L. Tan & H. H. Teh

Preliminary Study of the CPU Performance of the TITAN
Compared with that of the Cray X-MP/1   188
    E. Misaki, K.-M. Lue & R. Mendez

Reading List   203

Author Index   206

Seminar Opening Address

Dr Yashutada Uemura
Director
Japan Society for the Promotion of Science

Good Morning fellow participants !

On the occasion of this seminar organised under the joint auspices of the National University of Singapore (NUS) and the Japan Society for the Promotion of Science (JSPS), I would like to say a few words on behalf of JSPS.

First of all, I would like to extend a heartfelt welcome to all of you and hope that you will have a productive time in your academic discussions and that you will enjoy your pleasant stay in Tokyo.

I have heard that Singapore recognises the importance of information science and technology as well as applications to various kinds of industry as a key to national development. I also know that Singapore has already made great efforts in this direction.

As to the NUS - JSPS scientist exchange program, results in the field of computer science have accrued steadily year by year through the efforts of both core universities, the University of Singapore and the University of Tokyo. There can be no doubt, then, that holding a seminar on "Super Computer" at this time is very timely, since super computers are expected to contribute greatly to the advancement of various fields of science and technology.

So far, JSPS has supported six seminars in such fields as zoology, botany, chemistry and mathematics under the NUS - JSPS exchange program. In the fiscal year 1988, we are sponsoring two; one being this seminar and the other on "The Chemistry of Medically Used Plants".

I hope this seminar will contribute to the further advancement of scientific cooperation between both countries and even to prove a starting point for new developments.

This much said in a formal capacity, I will ask your permission to express my rather personal sentiments this morning. I now recall a Japanese computer scientist, Dr Hidetoshi Takahashi, late Prof. Emeritus of the University of Tokyo, who passed away several years ago. He was a physicist by background, but was really the pioneer of computer science in Japan, the key person at the beginning of the Department of Information Science and of the Computer Center of the University of Tokyo. He constructed the first solid state electronic computer in Japan by using a ferrite core in 1958 soon after the discovery of its parametric memory capacity in 1954 by one of his graduate student at that time, now Prof. Eiichi Goto. Many Japanese participants in this seminar are direct or indirect recipients of his academic influence. I think of him as the epitome of a man who loves and enjoys his life in scientific research. I am very sorry that we do not have him among our distinguished participants today.

Last but not least, I would like to express my sincere thanks to the organisers on both sides, Prof. Eiichi Goto, the University of Tokyo, Prof. Yuen Chung Kwong, the National University of Singapore, and all the members of the organising committee for dealing with the preparatory work so efficiently so as to realise this seminar.

Thank you.

30 May 1988

Part 1
Supercomputer Application in the Natural Sciences

Flow Simulation on Supercomputer

Application of Super-Computers in Weather Prediction

An Introduction to Atmospheric General Circulation Model (Abstract)

Satellite Remote Sensing Applications

A Supercomputer-Based Neural Network Simulating System

Flow Simulation on Supercomputer

Kunio Kuwahara
The Institute of Space and Astronautical Science,
Yoshinodai, Sagamihara, kanagawa 229, Japan

Recent development of supercomputers has enabled to compute flow field using the grid system with the order of 100x100x100 points; this number of grid points may not be sufficient to analyse a turbulent boundary layer but is good for laminar boundary layer.

In this paper, we show some typical results of flow simulation on supercomputer.

In the References, papers are listed on other simulations.

Method of Computation

The unsteady imcompressible full Navier-Stokes equations written in generalized coordinates are solved directly without any turbulence model. All spatial derivatives except those of nonlinear terms are approximated by central difference for incompressible flow. The nonlinear terms are approximated by a third-order upwind scheme. This scheme has a numerical diffusion approximately expressed by fourth-order derivative.

The computational schemes for compressible flow in the References are based on the implicit factored method with improved accuracy. Artificial diffusion term of fourth-order difference is added in the explicit term, as is usually done, to remove the aliasing errors and to stabilize the computation.

For the convective terms in the right-hand side, fourth-other differencing is used in order to improve the accuracy in the inviscid region. The Jacobian and the metric terms are also formed by using fourth-order differencing.

Examples

1) Circular Cylinder

In order to caputure the drag crisis, the flow was computed at Reynolds numbers 200000 and 400000. Figure 1 is the computed pressure contours which clearly show the difference of the flow patterns before and after the drag crisis. The number of grid points is 1000x100. From this computation it can be said that the present method is suited to capture the characteristics of high Reynolds number flows.

2) Sphere

The unsteady flow fields around a sphere are presented in Figs.2 and 3. Time development of pressure contour shows the mechanism of vortex shedding. Unstable flow patterns are recognized at the immediate leeward area of separation (Fig.2). Various fluctuations of pressure distributions on the surface of a sphere manifest that instability generates wavy patterns over the circumfrence of the vortex rings.

3) Slant-based body of revolution

Flow around a slant-based body of revolution with its axis aligned parallel to the uniform flow at Reynolds mumber Re=10^5 is investigated. The dependence of the drag coefficient on the slant base angle is found to be in satisfactory quantitative agreement with the experimental data (Fig.4). In particular, the drastic jump of the drag coefficient arround the critical base angle, α_c, is captured successfully.

Extensive flow visualizations, using the computed results, have been made on two distinct separation patterns. When the base angle is smaller than α_c, the separation pattern is of the quasi-axisymmetric dead water type (Fig.5). On the other hand, when the base angle is greater than α_c, the flow is characterized by a "U"-shaped vortex tube which originates from the base surface. In the wake structure of the latter case, a region of strong negative pressures appears on the upper-half edge of the base surface.

Conclusion

Owing to the development supercomputers, computational fluid dynamics has come to the stage where it can predict these detailed structure of high Reynolds number flows, not only in 2D but also in 3D by direct integration of the Navier-Stokes equations. These phenomena have not been able to be or have been very difficult to be observed by experiments.

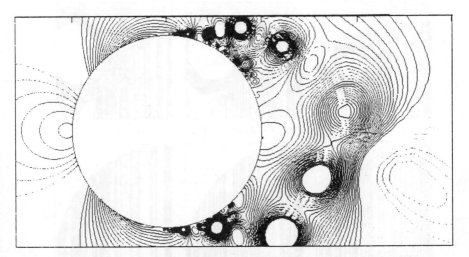

(a) Reynolds number 200000.

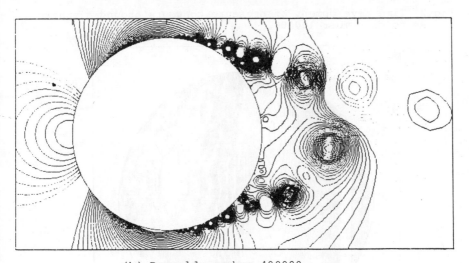

(b) Reynolds number 400000.

Fig.1 Pressure contours of a flow past
a 2-D circular cylinder.

6

(a) On the body surface and center plane.

(b) Enlarged ones on the body surface.

Fig.2 Time development of pressure contours around a sphere.
Reynolds number 100000.

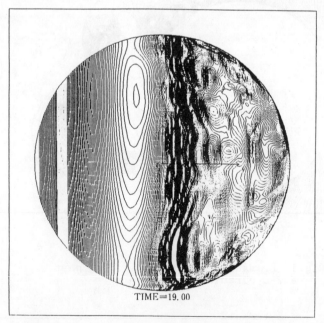

TIME=19.00

Fig.3 Instantaneous pressure distribution on the surface
of a sphere at Reynolds number 100000.

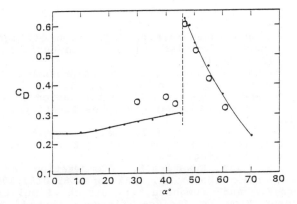

Fig.4 Drag coefficient variation with the slant base angle.
The solid line indicates the experimental results by Morel,
the present results are denoted by open circles.

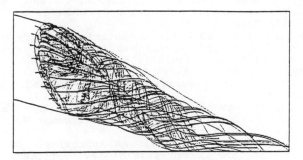

Fig.5(a) Instantaneous stream lines in the wake.
The slant base angle is 40 degrees.

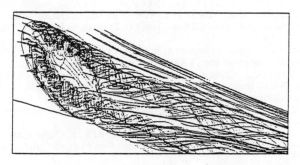

Fig.5(b) Instantaneous stream lines in the wake.
The slant base angle is 50 degrees.

8

References

(1) Kawamura,T. and Kuwahara,K.: Computation of High Reynolds Number Flow around a Circular Cylinder with Surface Roughness, AIAA Paper 84-0340, 1984.

(2) Ishii,K. Kuwahara,K.: Computation of Compressible Flow around a Circular Cylinder, AIAA Paper 84-1631,1984.

(3) Obayashi,S. and Kuwahara,K.: LU Factorization of an implicit Scheme for the Compressible Navier-Stokes Equations, AIAA Paper 84-1670,1984.

(4) Kuwahara,K.: Computation of Thermal Convection with a Large Temperature Difference, Proc.4th International Conference on Applied Numerical Modeling, 1984.

(5) Obayashi,S. and Kuwahara,K.: Computation of Unsteady Shock-Induced Vortex Separation, AIAA Paper 85-0183,1985.

(6) Kawamura,K. and Kuwahara,K.: Direct Simulation of a Turbulent Inner Flow by Finite-Difference Method, AIAA Paper 85-0376,1985.

(7) Shirayama,S.,Kuwahara,K. and Raul,M.,: A New Three-Dimensional Vortex Method, AIAA Paper 85-1488,1985.

(8) Himeno,R.,Kamo,K. and Kuwahara,K.: Computational Study of Three-Dimensional Wake Structure, AIAA Paper 85-1617,1985.

(9) Ishii,K.,Kuwahara,K.,Ogawa,S.,Chyu,W,J. and Kuwahara,K: Computation of Flow around a Circular Cylinder in a Supercritical Regime, AIAA Paper 85-1660,1985.

(10) Shida,Y. and Kuwahara,K.: Computational Study of Unsteady Compressible Flow around an Airfoil by a Block Pentadiagonal Matrix Scheme, AIAA Paper 85-1692,1985.

(11) Shirayama,S. and Kuwahara,K.: Computation of Flow past a Parachute by a Three-Dimensional Vortex Method, AIAA Paper 86-0350,1986.

(12) Takami,H. and Kuwahara,K.: Computation of the Dynamic Stall of an NACA0012 Airfoil by a Block Pentadiagonal Matrix Scheme, AIAA Paper 86-0116.1986.

(13) Obayashi,S. and Kuwahara,K.: An Approximate LU Factorization Method for the Compressible Navier-Stokes Equations, Journal of Computational Physics 63. pp157-167,1986.

(14) Kamo,K., Kubota,H.,Himeno,R. and Kuwahara,K.: Computational Simulation of the Flow Around a Rocket Body at High Angle of Attack, AIAA Paper 86-1778-cp,1986.

(15) Obayashi,S. and Kuwahara,K.: Navier-Stokes Simulation of Side Wall Effect of Two-Dimensional Transonic Wind Tunnel, AIAA Paper 87-0037,1987.

(16) Shirayama,S. and Kuwahara,K.: Patterns of Three-Dimensional Boundary Layer Separation, AIAA Paper 87-0461,1987.

(17) Shirayama,S., Ohota,T. and Kuwahara,K.: Three-Dimensional Flow past a Two-Dimensional Body, AIAA Paper 87-0605,1987.

(18) Shida,Y.,Kuwahara,K.,Ono,K. and Takami,H.: Computation of Dynamic Stall of a NACA-0012 Airfoil, AIAA Journal,Vol.25,-No.3.,1987.

(19) Hashiguchi,M.,Ohota,T. and Kuwahara,K.: Computational Study of Aerodynamic Behavior of a Car Configuration, AIAA Paper 87-1386,1987.

(20) Shida,Y. and Kuwahara,K.: Computation of Flow around an NACA0012 airfoil at High Angle of Attack, AIAA Paper 87-1425,-1987.

(21) Shirayama,S. and Kuwahara,K.: A Zonal Approach for Computation of Unsteady Incompressible Viscous Flow, AIAA Paper 87-1140-CP,1987.

(22) Tamura,T.,Kuwahara,K. and Shirayama,S.: Numerical Study of Unsteady Flow Patterns and Pressure Distributions on a Rectangular Cylinder, Proc.7th Int. Conf. on Wind Engineering,1987.

(23) Shirayama,S. and Kuwahara,K.: Computational Study of Flow in a Curved Pipe With Circular Cross Section, KSME Journal. Vol.1.No.1.pp.52-59,1987.

(24) Tamura,T., Tsuboi,K. and Kuwahara,K.: Numerical Simulation of Unsteady Flow Patterns around a Vibrating Cylinder, AIAA Paper 88-0128,1988.

(25) Kuwahara,K.,Shirayama,S. and Tamura,T.: Unsteady Vortex Shedding Behind a bluff body, Proc.12th World Congress on Scientific Computation,1988.

(26) Tamura,T.,Krause,E. and Kuwahara,K.: Three-dimensional Computation of Unsteady Flows around a Square Cylinder, Proc.11th ICNMFD,1988.

(27) Tsuboi,K., Shirayama,S., Oana,M. and Kuwahara,K.: Computational Study of the Effect of Base Slant, Proc. Second Int. conf. on Supercomputing in the Automotive Industry,1988.

APPLICATION OF SUPER-COMPUTERS IN WEATHER PREDICTION

Lim Hock

Department of Physics
National University of Singapore
Kent Ridge, Singapore 0511
Republic of Singapore

ABSTRACT

The scientific problem of numerical weather prediction (NWP) is basically one of simulating the circulation of the atmosphere, taking into consideration the thermal effects of solar and terrestrial radiations, latent heat exchange with water in its phase changes, and interactions with the underlying land and oceanic surface. Operational implementation of NWP also depends on close international cooperation and efficient telecommunications so that the initial condition of the atmosphere could be defined in good time. Supercomputers are essential in enabling a forecast to be computed within about six hours of the observation time. For large-scale atmospheric circulations, NWP has out-performed human forecasters since 1960s, and is now capable of producing useful forecast to about seven days in the temperate latitudes and to about three days in the tropical regions.

1. A BRIEF HISTORY OF NUMERICAL WEATHER PREDICTION

In 1904, V. Bjerknes formulated the problem of weather prediction as an initial-value problem in fluid dynamics. He however recognised two difficulties in putting his idea into practice:

- the equations were highly non-linear and did not have closed solutions, except possibly in grossly simplified forms that had little relevance to weather prediction;

- data available were far from adequate for determining the initial conditions.

The first attempt in calculating a weather prediction was made during the first world war, by L. F. Richardson[1]. He derived finite-difference approximations to the fluid dynamic equations and set out to compute a 24-hour prediction of weather over central Europe. Using desk calculators, he spent one year to complete the project but the result was a complete failure. His forecast of surface pressure changes were at least one order of magnitude too large. However, convinced of the validity of his approach, he published his work in 1922. He envisaged that weather prediction could one day be computed real-time by a team of mathematicians in a well orchestrated, factory-like "production line." He estimated that about 60,000 mathematicians working round-the-clock would be able to keep pace with actual weather development (rather optimistic an estimate, it now appears).

From today's vintage point, the reasons of his failure are clear: poor data for definition of the initial condition; faulty finite difference equations which suffered from computational instability; the needless physical complexity of the equations he used, which described not only motions relevant to weather, but also all sort of "noise" such as acoustic waves.

It took another twenty years of technological and theoretical development before numerical weather prediction (NWP) became a reality. In 1928, Courant, Friedrichs, and Lewy[2] discovered the criterion for numerical stability of finite difference equations. In the 1940s, a hierarchy of NWP models were derived based on careful analyses of the atmospheric dynamics. In these models, processes irrelevant to weather were removed, so that the dynamics of weather could be better understood and computational effort greatly reduced. Meanwhile, development in telecommunications enabled world-wide observations to be collected at major weather centres within a few hours of observation time. The widespread use of balloons for weather observations also began to provide a three-dimensional view of the atmospheric circulations. Finally, the electronic computers came on the scene in late 1940s.

Weather prediction was one of the problems John von Neumann had in mind for his newly invented electronic computers. During 1949–50, he worked with two meteorologists, J. G. Charney and R. Fjørtoft[3], to produce the first successful weather prediction on the ENIAC. The NWP model they used was a two-dimensional vorticity equation equation over a limited area. What they did has become a standard junior undergraduate project in meteorology courses nowadays, and can be easily repeated on an IBM PC. However, it took ENIAC one whole day to compute a one-day forecast. The five forecasts they computed were judged to be comparable in accuracy to those produced by highly skilled human forecasters using subjective methods.

John von Neumann's experiment was observed with great interest by the American Weather Bureau, Air Force and Navy. In 1954, these organisations jointly started the first routine NWP operation. This was followed after a few years by the United Kingdom, and then Japan. By late 1970s, all advanced countries had adopted NWP as the basis of their weather prediction services. During 1980s, developing countries also began computerisation of their weather services and experimenting with NWP.

2. THE SCIENTIFIC PROBLEM

Assuming the atmosphere to be a layer of ideal gas over a globe, the following equations would serve as a basis for predicting its behaviour:

$$\frac{\partial \mathbf{V}}{\partial t} + \mathbf{V} \cdot \nabla \mathbf{V} + 2\Omega \times \mathbf{V} + \frac{1}{\rho}\nabla p = \mathbf{g} + \mathbf{F}$$

$$\frac{\partial \rho}{\partial t} + \nabla \cdot (\rho \mathbf{V}) = 0$$

$$c_v \left(\frac{\partial}{\partial t} + \mathbf{V} \cdot \nabla\right) T - p\left(\frac{\partial}{\partial t} + \mathbf{V} \cdot \nabla\right)\rho^{-1} = Q$$

$$p = \rho R T$$

where $\mathbf{V}$ denotes the vector wind speed, $\mathbf{g}$ the vector gravitational acceleration, Ω the vector angular velocity of the earth's spin, c_v the specific heat of air at constant volume, and p, ρ, T denote the pressure, density, temperature respectively of an air parcel. The term Q in the third equation includes heating by solar radiation, and heat exchange with the underlying ocean or land surface; the term $\mathbf{F}$ represents mainly the frictional effect near the lower boundary of the atmosphere. The equations are to be solved subject to the boundary condition that no flow is allowed through the atmosphere-land (could be highly irregular) and atmosphere-ocean interface.

The above model is not adequate for prediction of weather. In the real atmosphere, one constituent — water — changes phase from vapour to liquid to solid, with accompanying release or absorption of a large quantity of heat. Condensed water in the form of cloud changes the transfer of radiation in the atmosphere, and snow and ice covers change the surface albedo and the heat exchange between the atmosphere and the earth's surface. For accurate prediction of weather, it is necessary to add another set of equations describing the earth's hydrological cycle. During the last decade or so, it has also become clear that it will be necessary to couple the atmospheric equations with a full ocean circulation model to take into account the complicated interactions between air and ocean, and to compute soil moisture and conductivity, in order to extend the useful forecast range beyond about 10 days.

From another point of view, the equations as listed above are too complicated. They describe not only motions directly relevant to weather, but also gravity waves and acoustic waves. Due to the Courant-Friedrichs-Lewy condition for numerical stability, even super-computers will not be able to compute fast enough for the purpose of weather prediction using the above equations. In the earlier NWP models, acoustic and gravity waves were removed by reformulating the equations. The current NWP models normally exclude only acoustic waves. For accurate forecast of tropical and smaller scale weather phenomena, it is necessary to take into account the effects of gravity waves.

As to the numerical solution techniques, most of the early models used finite-difference methods. The current global NWP models are mostly spectral models. In spectral models, the variables are expanded in terms of spherical harmonics for computation of the linear terms. Interactions among the harmonic components are computed in the real space and efficiently transformed to the harmonic space using a combination of fast Fourier transform and Gaussian quadrature techniques.

NWP models for prediction of smaller-scale weather phenomena are mostly finite-difference models. Recently, finite element models with semi-Lagrangian advection schemes have been experimented and found to be very successful.

All these models provide at best a rather fuzzy view of the atmosphere. For instance, a typical finite-difference global model has grid-points spaced at about 100 km apart. Violent small-scale weather systems such as thunderstorms have dimensions of about 30 km and are not represented at all on such a sparse grid. These important small-scale weather systems have to be treated as "turbulence" in the global flow pattern. The parameterization of their important dynamic and thermal effects remains a major research area in the science of NWP. A comprehensive introduction to the techniques and research interests of NWP is provided by the textbook by Haltiner and Williams[4].

3. THE LOGISTIC PROBLEMS

Before NWP can be implemented on a routine basis, many logistic problems have to be solved. First, there must be good observational data to define the initial state. Under the

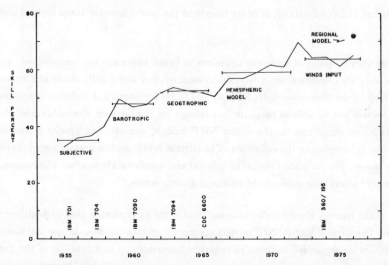

Fig. 1 Record of skill, averaged annually, of the 36-hour forecast of the 500-mb (about 5.6 km high) circulation issued by the National Meteorological Center of the United States of America. Note the increase in skill score with every upgrade of computer and NWP model. (Source: F. G. Schuman, *Numerical weather prediction* in *Geophysical Predictions*, National Academy of Sciences, Washington, D. C., 1978.)

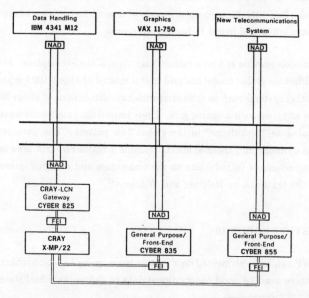

Fig. 2 Configuration of the computer complex of the European Centre for Medium Range Weather Forecast around 1986.

NAD   Network Access Device
FEI   Front-End Interface
——   High Speed Data Highway (Control Data LCN)
═══   Dedicated Channel Connections

coordination of the World Meteorological Organization, surface and upper air conditions are observed and reported simultaneously four times a day all over the world. These weather reports are sent through dedicated telecommunications network so that major weather centres will receive all the reports within four hours of observation time. Front-end computers intercept these report, check for obvious errors and request for retransmission of corrupted reports.

The received data are the processed by an objective analysis system which produces a three-dimensional structure of the atmosphere from the irregularly scattered observations.

The consistency between the different dynamic variables — temperature, wind, pressure, etc., — is then checked. Adjustments in the objective analyses are made so that the dynamic variables, when taken together, constitute a plausible state of the atmosphere, consistent with known dynamical constraints. This step of processing is often called initialisation.

The initialised data are then fed into NWP systems to produce forecasts. The forecast results are further customised to meet the need of users. At this stage, as well as the analysis and initialisation processes, advanced graphic and image facilities are essential. To derive the full benefit from the forecast, smooth communication and mutual understanding between the forecast offices and the users plays an important part.

4. SUCCESSES, RESEARCH AREAS, AND THE NEED FOR SUPER-COMPUTERS

Fig. 1 shows the improving skill of NWP at the National Meteorological Center of the United States from mid-1950s to mid-1970s. Data for the period mid-1970s to mid-1980s are unfortunately not neatly summarised as in Fig. 1; but from scattered reports, the trend of improving skill with each upgrade of computer and NWP model continues.

After more than 30 years of research and development, NWP has put the practice of weather prediction firmly on the basis of scientific principles. NWP has long since out-performed human forecasters. The period of useful forecast has been extended from about two days in the pre-NWP era to about seven days for large scale weather events in the temperate latitudes, and from one day to about three days (provided good data is available for definition of the initial conditions) in the tropical region. Intensive effort is now focused on medium range (one to four weeks) weather prediction.

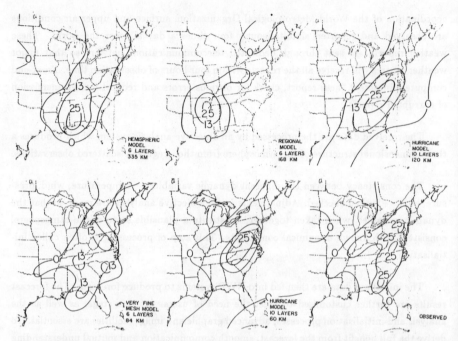

Fig. 3 Prediction of precipitation amount in mm during the last 12 hours of a 48-hour forecast. The forecasts obtained using models with 335-km and 168-km grid lengths are quite misleading; whereas the forecasts obtained using models with 84-km and 60-km grid lengths are acceptable. The observed distribution is given at the lower right corner. Note that the 60-km grid length model has 10 vertical levels while the 84-km grid length model has only 6 vertical levels. (Source: F. G. Schuman, *Numerical weather prediction* in *Geophysical Predictions*, National Academy of Sciences, Washington, D. C., 1978.)

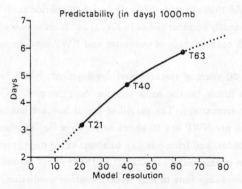

Fig. 4 Skill of forecasts made with a spectral model of ECMWF with different resolutions, T21(low) to T63 (high). The number of days to which useful forecasts were obtained increased from three to six days as the resolution was increased.

A few scientific problems still awaits satisfactory solutions. A break-through in the parameterisation of convection may be expected to bring with it a quantum leap in forecast skill, especially for the tropical region. Much attention is now devoted to a proper treatment of the surface orography. New numerical techniques are being experimented to better represent the barrier effects of steep mountains.

In these efforts, computer power has always been a limiting factor. To produce a forecast in good time, all the computations, NWP as well as the pre- and post-processing, have to be completed within a few fours after the time observations are made. In advanced countries, NWP are often implemented with fast "number crunchers." The computers indicated in Fig. 1 are all "supercomputers" of their time, e.g., IBM 360/195 in the 1970s. Fig. 2 shows the computer system of the European Centre for Medium Range Weather Forecast (ECMWF) at around 1986, where a CRAY X-MP/22 is linked through a loosely-coupled network to various functional front-end computers.

The potential benefit of having powerful computers is clearly highlighted in Figs. 3 and 4. Fig. 3 is about 10 years old. It shows how the forecast of precipitation amount over the eastern United States improved with increasing resolution of the model, which means also geometrically increasing computational effort. Fig. 4 is from a recent report (1985) of ECMWF. It shows that by increasing the resolution of a spectral model, the predictability range is extended from three days to six days.

Meteorologists are aware that for a highly nonlinear system like the atmosphere, there is probably an inherent limit to the predictability to its behaviour. In fact, it was an eminent meteorologist, E. N. Lorenz, who first discovered a "strange attractor" of a chaotic system in his research into the predictability problem[5]. Theoretical estimates put the limit at about two weeks which many researchers feel might be a little pessimistic. Anyway, experiments such as those shown in Figs. 3 and 4 shows that although much basic improvement is still necessary, the present NWP models are capable of higher forecast skill if computer power allows higher resolutions to be used in routine operational NWP.

This requirement on ever larger computer power is likely to remain in the near future. Despite the predictability theory of atmospheric circulations, meteorologists are hopeful that useful forecasts for 30 days to 2–3 years time scale may still be possible. Such long range forecasts will not provide local details as in short range predictions, but will give indications of the general trends over regional weather/climate conditions. This is not wishful thinking. The basis for such optimism are the observations that atmospheric

18

events of such time scales are often not freely evolving but are subject to forcings by outside mechanisms, such as the feedback from the tropical oceans which evolve very much more slowly than the atmosphere. El Ñino, a phenomenon that has recently been given some publicity, is an example of the atmospheric events under consideration. Atmosphere-ocean coupled models will be the proper tool for prediction of such events. The attendant increase in the demand for computer power could only be met probably with the next generation of supercomputers.

REFERENCES

1. Richardson, L. F., *Weather Prediction by Numerical Process*, Cambridge University Press, London, 236pp, (1922). (Dover reprint, New York, 1965).

2. Courant, R., K. O. Friedrichs, and H. Lewy, *Über die partiellen differenzengleichungen der mathematischen Physik*, Math. Ann., **100**, 32, (1928).

3. Charney, J. G., J. Fjørtoft, and John von Neumann, *Numerical integration of the barotropic vorticity equation*, Tellus, **2**, 237–254, (1950).

4. Haltiner, G. J. and R. T. Williams, *Numerical Prediction and Dynamic Meteorology*, John Wiley and Sons, Inc., New York, 477pp, (1980).

5. Lorenz, E. N., *Deterministic nonperiodic flow*, J. Atmos. Sci., **20**, 130–141, (1963).

AN INTRODUCTION TO ATMOSPHERIC GENERAL CIRCULATION MODEL

Tatsushi Tokioka

Meteorological Research Institute, Tsukuba, Ibaraki 305, Japan

ABSTRACT

An outline of atmospheric general circulation model (GCM) is presented with special emphasis on its mathematical and computational aspects. A model is based on physical laws, such as hydrodynamic equations, the first law of thermodynamics, continuity equation, equation of state and conservation of several materials. Sub-grid-scale processes , such as cumulus convections, boundary layer turbulence, and sub-grid-scale diffusions are parameterized and incorpolated in the model.

To express fields on the sphere, either a grid method or a spectral method is used. Spherical harmonic functions are used in the latter. In the vertical direction, the atmosphere is divided into layers.

At present, atmospheric GCM is not much different from a numerical forecasting model. However, more effort has been paid in the former to simulate statistical behaviour of atmospheric flows. On the other hand, the latter concerns local accuracy of the flows more than the former does, i.e. spatial resolution is very important for a numerical forecasting model.

The model can be divided into two parts, i.e., adiabatic process of the flows and diabatic process. The latter includes radiative heating of solar and terrestrial radiation, heating due to condensations, turbulent heat flux convergence, energy and momentum exchanges with the lower boundary surface, etc. Each process is integrated with a different time increment, i.e., one to three hours for diabatic process and a much shorter time increment for adiabatic one. In order to simulate global scale flows in a stable way, such a small increment of time has to be used even for a long-term integration over a year. To economize time integrations, many suitable methods are developed in this field, such as semi-implicit method and split-explicit method.

Computations in adiabatic process can be economized in vector processor machines, however computations in diabatic process can hardly be improved by the use of vector processor machine due to the nature of the process, such as a treatment of clouds in radiation calculation and cumulus convections. To economize this part, parallel processor machine has

20

to be used.

Currently a climate model is being developed, where an atmospheric GCM is combined with an oceanic GCM. The model is designed to predict almost all climatological elements based on physical, chemical and possibly biological laws or processes. This kind of model is urgently needed to predict or assess possible changes of climate or its fluctuations which might arise from many causes including human activities. For such purposes, speed of a computer is required to be 10 GFLOPS at least.

SATELLITE REMOTE SENSING APPLICATIONS

Y.J. Chong

Department of Physics

Natonal University of Singapore

Republic of Singapore 0511

ABSTRACT

In the applications of satellite remote sensing, it is often necessary to generate a geo-coded composite image from the data acquired by different remote sensing satellites. The use of a supercomputer would enable this enormous task to be performed accurately and in a timely manner. This would open up many new possibilities of applications of satellite remote sensing.

1. INTRODUCTION

A large number of artificial earth-orbiting satellites, including meteorological, environmental and earth resources satellites are daily gathering data concerning the land and sea surface of the earth. There is a growing awareness of the power of using such remote sensing data for the study of a wide variety of environmental problems on earth.

2. REMOTE SENSING SATELLITES

The current interest in remote sensing may be said to have begun with the launching of Landsat-1 by NASA on July 23 1972. Landsat-1 became inactive on January 6 1978. Currently Landsat-4 and Landsat-5 are in operation.

On 22 February 1986, France's C.N.E.S. launched the first of its own series of remote sensing satellites, SPOT-1; and on 19 February 1987, Japan's National Space Development Agency launched the Marine Observation Satellite, MOS-1.

In the next few years more remote sensing satellites will be launched. Among these will be:

> European Remote Sensing Satellite (ERS-1)
> Japanese Earth Resources Satellite (JERS)
> Canadian Radarsat
> Advanced Earth Observation Satellite (ADEOS)

It has been estimated that by 1992, the International Space Year, at least 14 remote sensing satellites could be expected to be in orbit performing passive acquisition of remote sensing data in the visible and infrared region as well as active acquisition of remote sensing data in the microwave region.

3. ACQUISITION OF SATELLITE DATA

Within the Association of South East Asian Nations, (ASEAN), which comprises Brunei, Indonesia, Malaysia, Philippines, Singapore and Thailand, there are several satellite ground receiving stations. This has made it possible for the ASEAN countries to receive a wide variety of remote sensing data from Landsat, SPOT, and MOS as well as from the meteorological NOAA satellites.

4. COMPUTER PROCESSING OF SATELLITE DATA

The data obtained by a satellite sensor contain information on the amount of
radiant energy reflected (or emitted) by the land or sea surface within a
particular band of the electromagnetic spectrum. To be suitable for
applications such data would have to be processed by computer image
processing techniques in order to make them more easily interpretable by the
ultimate user.

5. REQUIREMENTS OF DATA USERS

The capability to process the acquired remote sensing data effectively and
in a timely manner is an extremely important factor for the successful
application of remote sensing technology. Appropriate methods of handling
and processing of the data would have to be developed in order to present
them in a suitable form that would meet the requirements of the applications
users.

One of the most important requirements of users is the availability of a
cloud-free image in a timely manner. A common experience of the ASEAN
countries is the frequent presence of extensive cloud cover over the region.
It is not often that a satellite overpass coincides with a clear sky over a
particular area. This renders the acquisition of a good cloud-free image
very difficult. The long wait for a cloud-free image from any one particular
satellite would rule out many potential applications of remote sensing.

6. GENERATION OF COMPOSITE IMAGE

One solution to overcome this would be to form a composite image from the
cloud-free portions of different images acquired at different times by a
variety of different remote sensing satellites.

However the images acquired by different satellite sensors have different characteristics such as for example pixel alignment, spatial resolution and spectral range.

To generate a useful composite image the different characteristics of each satellite sensor must be taken into account. The data from each satellite sensor would have to be geocoded into a standard format.

The principal advantage of a geocoded image is that it can be directly overlayed on other geocoded images of the same area made from the data of different satellites. An accurate and meaningful composite image can then be obtained by eliminating the cloud covered portions of each individual image and superimposing the geocoded images from the different satellites on each other.

7. GEOCODING OF DATA

In order to perform geocoding of an image for a particular area of interest, an appropriate cartographic projection of the area with a suitable scale is first chosen. For each raw image acquired by a specific satellite sensor, a geometric transformation and resampling of the data is undertaken in order to produce a new image in this projection and with this scale. This has to be carried out with the minimal loss of radiance information for each picture element (pixel) in the new geocoded image.

8. VECTOR COMPILERS

The radiance value of a pixel in an image depends on its column and its row in the image, as well as on the electromagnetic band. It is thus an array in three variables. Geocoding involves three nested do-loops. The availability of vector compilers in supercomputers would speed up this process considerably.

9. PARALLEL PROCESSING

A distinguishing feature of supercomputers is the parallel processing capability that they provide. Parallel processing would enable the geocoding of the data of different satellites to be performed simultaneously thereby speeding up considerably the generation of a composite image.

The delineation of changes in the environment over a period of time can also be performed very effectively by parallel processing of data acquired at different times.

10. CONCLUSION

The availability of parallel processing, vector compilers, and high-speed data access and storage in a supercomputer would enable the enormous task of generating a geocoded composite image from the data of different satellites to be performed more accurately and in a more timely manner. This would open up many new exciting possibilities of applications of satellite remote sensing and pave the way for the successful implementation of satellite remote sensing in the the countries of South East Asia.

A Supercomputer-Based Neural Network Simulating System

K F Loe   L S Hsu   S C Chan   and H B Low[t]
Deparment of Information Systems and Computer Science
† Instiute of System Science
National University of Singapore
Kent Ridge, Singapore 0511

Abstract

In this paper we propose the implementation of a neural network simulating system to be executed in a supercomputer. Though computer architectures of massively parallel neurocomputer do not bear any similarity with the supercomputers, the availability of large memory and the power of number crunching of supercomputer make it a good tool for simulating the computational process of neurocomputer. The knowledge processing of neurocomputers is basically analogue in nature and involves a lot of numerical iterations. A large memory is required to store the structures of the neural network even for a small neural network. Our simulating system consists of a language called HTNSL. A preprocessor will translate the statements of this language into a general high level language suitable for the target supercomputer. HTNSL is an object oriented langauge and it includes statements which by nature of the langauge design are suitable for parallel processing. However the degree of implementable parallelism depends on the target supercomputer.

1. Introduction

The current interest of artificial intelligence is based mainly on the assumption that the brain is a symbolic computation machine. The physiology structure of brain is immaterial in this approach to the study of intelligence. The main concern is to understand the high level cognitive behaviour of intelligence so as to implement in the traditional computer system having knowledge stored symbolically in the computer memory. Lisp and later also Prolog are widely used in programming the intelligence system since these languages are very suitable for manipulating symbols. Another approach in exploring the intelligence is to look below the symbolic level to the microscopic level in order to understand how neurons and their connections are related to intelligent behaviours of human and other animals. In this approach to the study of intelligence, a new kind of computer architectures is necessary. This kind of computer is massively parallel and analogue in nature. Furthermore it is not easy to pinpoint exactly where the knowledge is stored, the knowledge is in fact distributed over the whole network as a kind of numerical constraints. Intelligence is manifested during the dynamic operation of the network.

With the advent of VLSI there are growing interests to build the neurocomputer. Simulation technique is the best we can do prior to such a design. Neurophysiology told us that the number of neurons in our brain is in the order of 10^{10}. At the current stage it is not only impossible to understand the complexity of such a system, but also we do not have the computational power to study such a complexity. Current studies of neural network are mainly done by simulation in the conventional computer systems. The bottleneck of such simulation systems is due to the memory size and the speed of computation. In fact the speed of processing of the individual neuron in the brain is slow. However the massively parallel processing of the neurons achieves the speed of knowledge processing far beyond any supercomputer we know to date. The current interest of modelling the neural network are based on the general framework of Parallel Distributed Processing (PDP) made well known by Rumelhart and McClelland[1]. In PDP most of the knowledge processing are numerical rather than symbolic, this is shown to be the case in learning or relaxation process so as to change the numerical weighting factors of the connections. A PDP simulating system called P3 has already been developed by D.ZIPSER and RABIN and implemented in LISP running in the SYMBOLICs 3600 LISP machine[1]. In view of the bottelneck of number crunching we have mentioned earlier, our conviction is that a supercomputer-based PDP simulating system shall be able to extend the scope and the scale of study of the PDP system. In our design we shall provide a system in which the user only required to provide a high level description of his model using HTNSL(Hierachical Type Neural Simulating Language). A preprocessor shall translate this language into the target language of the supercomputer.

Section 2 is an introduction to PDP model of neural network. Section 3 describes the langauge features of the simulating system and the operational environment which facilitate the implementation of parallel processing. Section 4 is an example illustrating the application of HTNSL for modelling a neural network.

2. Principles of PDP Approach

The details of PDP approach to neural network modelling can be found in [1]. We shall provide a brief description of PDP here. In PDP there is a set of processing units which models the neurons in the brain. Units in PDP can be classified into three categories namely the input, the output and the hidden units. Input units receive inputs from external source, output units send the processing result out of the system and the hidden units which lay between the input units and output units performs learning and knowledge processing. These units connect amongst themselves to form some patterns of connections. The output signal from a unit is fan-out to some adjacent units through the connections from this unit. Between any two units, there is a strength of connection which usually refers to as the weight between the two units; denoted as w_{ij} for connection between unit i and unit j. These weights are analogue to the sypnases' connection amongst neurons in the brain. At any given time t this set of unit possesses a set of activation values denoted as $a_i(t)$. Such a set of values represents the state of the system at time t. In some models of PDP the activation values are a set of discrete values such as $\{-1,0,1\}$; in another models they may possess continuous bounded or unbounded values. The output of a unit depends on its activation value. Such a dependency is described by a threshold function f as denoted by $o_i = f_i(a_i(t))$, where o_i is the output of unit i (sometime we call this operation as threshold logic operation).

The pattern of connections of the set of units in the PDP model is very important; it decides how the network stores its information and how it responds to an input information. A unit receives a set of inputs from some adjacent units which form a fan-in connection to the input of this unit. The output of this unit again would have a fan-out connection to other units. If an input to a unit is to enhance the activation of this unit the preceding unit which feeds input value to this unit is called the excitatory unit; otherwise it is an inhibitory unit to this unit. If there is a set of units(from 1 to j) which is activated at time t and it provides inputs to a unit i through a matrix of connection weight w_{ij}, then the propagation of activation value to unit i at time $(t+1)$ is given by,

$$a_i(t+1) = F(\sum_j w_{ij} o_j)$$

where F is a function properly selected by a modeller. The knowledge of a PDP model is actually stored in the connecting weights w_{ij} of the network.

The knowledge is acquired through learning. The learning process is roughly like this: the system is repeatedly impinged with a set of knowledge which the system is supposed to learn. The learning is through a learning rule which modifies the weight of the connection incrementally by an amount of Δw_{ij}. A general rule for learning is given by

$$\Delta w_{ij} = g(a_i(t), t_i(t)) h(o_j(t), w_{ij})$$

where $t_i(t)$ is a kind of teaching input to the unit i (if there is no teacher $t_i(t)$ is omitted). Also g and h are some functions which are contrived by the modeller. Finally we shall note that the environment of PDP is characterized by a probability distribution for a set of input patterns. Depending on the models, some PDP models may have restrictions on the kind of patterns the system can learn, another models may not have such restrictions.

3. Langauge of the Simulating System

HTNSL is a special purpose langauge for a user to code his neural network model. HTNSL adopts the same langauge design philosophy of HISDL which is a langauge for specifying the connection of computer circuitry[2]. However HISDL does not have the capability for specifying the behaviour of the system. Instead it only provides the connectivity description of a system which can be built-up hierarchically. HTNSL differs from HISDL in two main aspects: it is a simulation langauge and it can be used to specify the connectivity of sypnases in neural network. The input and output sypnases are always associated with the connection weights which complicate the specifications of the connection of sypnases.

HTNSL is an object oriented language. It has five types of type-definition namely Structure, Pattern, Block, Layer and Network. The functionality of the five type-definitions are different and they shall be explained in the following. All the type-specifications consists of three parts namely the header, the body and the delimiter.

3.1 Header and Delimiter

The header and the delimiter of the five type-definitions are shown as follows:

Structure

Endstructure

Pattern *<pattern—name >(parameter—list , io —spec)*

Endpattern

Block *<block—name >(parameter—list , io —spec)*

Endblock

Layer *<layer—name >(parameter—list , io —spec)*

Endlayer

Network *<network—name >(parameter—list , io —spec)*

Endnetwork

Structure is a collection of record types. After instantiated in Block, Layer or Network type, the record types can be used to access or update the data of the neural network. The data of the network are the values of each sypnase's weight, or the input and output values of the neural activation.

In modelling neural network, it is common that in a model there are some regular patterns of connections in a set of adjacent neurons which repeatedly appear throughout the entire network. The Pattern type in HTNSL is to facilitate such a description. Pattern can be instantiated in higher hierarchical type such as a Block.

A Block is an array of neurons having a set of patterns. Usually a Block has a boundary, when a Pattern is instantiated in the Block, those Pattern connections in the fringe of the Block would be cut-off by default of our system design but it is transparent to the user. It should be possible to implement an option so that the user can specify how he would like the system to handle the fringe connection of patterns. However it may require the user to have some knowledge of the internal design of HTNSL.

A Block is the only type which allows the user to build hierarchical Block, i.e. copies of named Block type can be instantiated into a Block type so as to form a higher hierarchical named Block type. Forming higher hierarchical Pattern type is not allowed, however Patterns can be instantiated in Block, so that instantiated Patterns overlap each other partially or fully.

Finally all the named Block types have to be instantiated into at least one of the Layer. Layer is necessary for updating the simulation clock, so that the activation of neurons in Blocks of the same Layer would be updated synchronously.

A collection of instantiated named Layer types forms a Network type which is a type for an overall system model. The order of connection of the instantiated Layers gives the proper order of simulation time propagation and the neural activation layer by layer. We define a cycle of neural network operation as the propagation of external input signal until the signal reaches the output of the network.

Following the type-definitions are the names of the types given by the user. They are denoted as <pattern-name>, <block-name> <layer-name> and <network-name> as given earlier. Structure does not have a user given name since in the body of Structure is a collection of types of records, and names will be given to each type of record in the body of Structure; thus a collective name for all type records is unneccesary.

Following the name of a type is the Parameter-list. Parameter-list is a set of parameters used in the body of the type being designed.

Immediately after the parameter-list is the io-spec. The io-spec includes specifications of input, output and bidirectional connections. To specify the input, output or bidirectional terminals, they are preceded by the syntax ">", "<" and "=" then followed by the respective terminal names. For example (< OUC, OST(r*r) , OWT(r|w), OCT(r*r|+w), ODT(r*r|+w|b)) specifies a set of output terminals. Here OUC is declared as a single output terminal. OST(r*r) is declared as an array of r*r output terminals so that OST(i,j) denotes an output terminal at location (i,j) of a Block(assuming OST is declared in a Block). OWT(r*r|w) is declared as an array output of r*r terminals and each terminal OWT(i,j) at location (i,j) has a weight w(i,j) associated with it. Therefore the activated output value at the immediate output location of the terminal and after the weighted connection location is different by a weighting factor. We use OWT(i,j) to denote the signal value

of immediate output from a neuron at location (i,j) and OWT(i,j|w) to denote
the output given by OWT(i,j|w)=OWT(i,j)*w(i,j), i.e. weighted output.
When OWT(r*r|+w) is declared as output terminals in the *io-spec* then
OWT(r*r|+w) denote the weighted-sum-output. The computation of the
weighted-sum-output is given in the Method section of a typed module. For
example in the Method may contain a statement like: OCT(r*r|+w) =
w(i,j)*OCT(i,j)**2 which means that w(i,j) multiplied by the squares of
OCT(i,j) and the product is summed from i=1 to r and j= 1 to r. The result
produces an output denoted by OCT(r*r|+w).

Finally the Endstructure, Endblock, Endlayer or Endnetwork is to delimit a module of
a named type.

The order of writing each of the named type module is immaterial. However
it is advisable to write the Structure first because a general skeleton of a model
is usually its data structure. If we write the Structure first it would be helpful
for writing other typed modules later.

Embedded within Structure and Endstructure is the body of the Structure type
which consists of statements for declaring the record types to be used in
other modules. Usually a record type is instantiated in other modules with
the dimensional parameters so that it can be used for accessing the weights
or the input/output values of neuron activation. For example if we put
PC(NW,UUC,UC,CSET) in between Structure and Endstructure then PC is the
name of a record type. The record attributes are NW,UUC,UC and CSET
which are also the names to be used latter for type-definitions. For instance,
if NW, UUC, UC and CSET are used as names for Network, Layer, Block and
Pattern type-definitions respectively then these record attributes can be used
to access the data of these typed modules.

3.2 Instance Connect and Method

The body of Network, Layer or Block consists of three optional parts namely
Instance, Connect and Method. As for Pattern type, it does not have Instance and
Connect parts and Method is the only optional part. For instance a Block type
with a name UC may contain Instance, Connect and Method in the following
format:

Block UC(r,--- >IC(r*r) ---)
Instance ---
Connect

Endconnect
Method

Endmethod
Endblock

By using Instance statement more complicated higher hierarchical types from some primitive types can be built. The above example of UC Block type could be constructed from some primitive types such as Pattern by making instances of Pattern type in UC using the Pattern statement. Again more complicated and higher hierarchical types such as Layer type or Block type of instantiated Block may also be constructed. An example of the instantiation of UC Block type into a Layer type with a name UUC is shown as follows:

Layer UUC(n,p, ---- >IMS(n) ----)
Instance UCI[n]:UC
Connect
For i=1,n
UCI[i](p > IMS[i] -----)
/OVC[i|wa] UUS.IAS[j]/
Endfor

Endlayer

The above Instance UCI[n]:UC creates n copies of UC instances with a given Instance name UCI so that any UCI[i] is a copy of UC.

After instantiation of copies of UC connections can be made. There are two ways to make connections; either we make the terminals of the instantiated copies to share the declared terminal names in the $io-spec$ of the current module under construction, or we use a statement:/----/ to specify the terminal connections between the current module and another module which is not an instantiated copy of the current module but it is of the same type and with the same hierarchical level as the current module under consideration. To illustrate these two ways of connection we refer to the

UUC Layer type described earlier. UUC consists of n input terminals as given by the declaration:>IMS(n) in the *io-spec*. The Connect statement follows by For iteration makes instances of connection using IMS[i]. Each input IMS[i](out of n) is a copy of input IC(r*r) declaring in UC, thus it is actually consists of p*p number of input terminals; where p is a parameter declared in the *parameter-list* of UUC and it is an instantiation of r. An example of making another type of connection as shown in UUC is: /OVC[i,wa] UUS.IAS[j]/ which means that a terminal OVC[i] via a weight "wa" is connected to the terminal IAS[j] of another layer UUS which has been defined or to be defined latter using the Layer type.

The FOR statement in HTNSL is similar to DO loop in FORTRAN, however, in order to simplify the coding by HTNSL, a FOR statement is allowed to specify a few levels of array nesting computations provided all these nestings cover the same set of array statements, otherwise a seperated pair of FOR and Endfor nesting statement is needed. For instance,

For i=1,N,3 ; j=1,N,3

Endfor

is considered as a double looping from 1 to N having a step increment of 3 and j index is for the inner loop.

After we have made instantiations and connections in a typed module, procedure for computation within this module can be coded and is defined in the Method of the module. Since most of the supercomputers use FORTRAN as their main language therefore we adopt FORTRAN-like statements for writing procedure so as to simplify the design of the preprocessor. However we have introduced three statements which are frequently used in neural network computation but they are not part of the conventional FORTRAN statements. Two of them have been mentioned previously, i.e. the weighted-sum-output computation and the FOR statement.

The third statement is called the ampersand statement. An ampersand statement is used in an array of record type, and before a record type can be used in the Method it has to be instantiated. A record type of HTNSL, which is created by Structure as mentioned earlier, is different from the record type of Pascal. The record type of HTNSL is used only for accessing two kinds of data namely the input/output activation values of the neurons, and the connection weights of the sypnases. The earlier example of PC(NW,UUC,UC,CSET) which was declared as Structure type, may instantiate with the following parameters in one of the typed module using Instance statement like: Instance PC(q,k,nl*nl,rl*rl) which means that in the NW Network there is q number of UUC Layer, in the UUC Layer there is k number of UC Block, in the UC Block there are nl*nl number of neurons arranged in array configuration and a CSET Pattern of size rl*rl is applied to these Blocks. Suppose that in the UUC Layer type module there is an $io-spec$ output terminal written as " < OVC(k|wa) " then an ampersand statement written as,

$$Lax = max[OVC\#PC(2,3,4,5,\&)]$$

means that Lax is to assign the value of the maximum neuron output in an area cover by a CSET pattern with size rl*rl at UUC layer 2 UC block 3 of location (4,5). Therfore the meaning of "&" here is to list all the neural output terminals OVC covered by the CSET Pattern and find the maximum output among them.

Another format of using ampersand statement which is a abbreviated form for DO loop statement in FORTRAN, i.e.

$$WA\#PC(2,3,4,5,\&) = WA\#PC(2,3,,4,5,\&)+0.5$$

The above statement means updating all the weight WA of sypnases cover by the CSET pattern at UUC layer 2, UC block 3 of location (4,5) by an amount of 0.5. If nestings are involved they may be written using multiple ampersands like,

$$WA\#PC(2,\&\&,\&\&\&,\&) = WA\#PC(2,\&\&,\&\&\&,\&).$$

This statement is to specify a nesting of weight updating, and &, &&, &&& corresponding to the nestings of innermost loop, middle loop and outer loop respectively.

3.3 Environment and Parallel Processing

A neural network model is specified by the user using HTNSL. When coding a neural model the user must have at least a Layer type. The Network type is the highest hierarchical type; there is actually only one Network to be declared by the user.

Usually the initailization of the system and the reading of system parameters are done by statements embedded in the Method of the Network module. The input and output interfaces of the neural network under simulation are files connected to the systems. They are specified by read statements. In neural network there are two phases of system operations: the learning mode and the operational mode. During the learning mode the weight factors of the sypnases are updated according to the learning process prescribed in the Method in one of the module. After the system reaches the stable stage, we can put it into the operational mode. If the neural network model is for pattern recognition, then in the operational mode the system would be able to recognize a pattern it has learnt. These two modes of operations and the selection of modes are done by the coding in the Method.

In the Method we can also specify the output data we wish to observe. Basically there are two types of output data we can observe. Firstly one may want to observe the change of values of the weight or the terminal output value with respect to the simulation clock time. Secondly one may want to observe the weights of a set of sypnases or neural activation values so as to understand their relative strengths. Display is a statement for accessing the neural network data for observation purposes.

Display *wa#PC* (1,1,1,2,1,2):timechart, would allow user to observe the change of the weight connected to a neuron at a location (1,1,(1,2),(1,2)) v.s. the simulation clock time.

Display *wa#PC* (1,1,1,2,&):barchart would allow user to observe the strength of the weight connected to neurons covered by the CSET Pattern which centres at location(1,1,(1,2)).

The PDP model of neural network by itself is a parallel system. However a simulating system of PDP may not be a parallel system. HTNSL is designed to emulate the parallelism in neural network as closely as possible in its language design. The idea of Layer type in HTNSL is to make the simulation system easy to implement the parallel processing in supercomputer so that all the neurons in a Layer can be updated in parallel; emulating the parallelism in PDP. In the lower level of operation every Pattern in a Block can process in parallel as well.

The records of Structure type using the ampersand statement for data manipulation can also be carried out in parallel in a layer. In fact such statements should be able to vectorize.

Though HTNSL explores the parallelism of PDP in its language design, to what extend and in what way our simulation system can implement parallel simulation still depends on the type of supercomputer. When the preproceesor is designed we shall consider how to match the parallel features in HTNSL to the parallel operation offered by the supercomputer we use.

4. An Example of Neural Network Modelling

To show the application of the HTNSL, we attempt in the following to describe a rather complex neural network model. This neural network model is proposed by Fukushima[3] and is called "neocognitron". It has capability to recognize visual stimulus patterns neither affected by shift in position nor by a small distortion in shape of the stimulus patterns. It also has self-organizing capability.

The structure of "neocognitron" was inspired by the visual nervous system of the vertebrate. It consists of an input layer U_0 followed by a cascade of modular structures, each of which is composed of two layers of cells. The first layer of the module consists of "S-cells", which correspond to simple cells or lower hypercomplex cells according to the classification of Hubel and Wiesel[4]. The author called it the S-layer and denote the S-layer in the l_{th} module as U_{Sl}. The second layer of the structure consists of "C-cells", which correspond to complex cells or higher order hypercomplex cells. It was called the C-layer and denoted by U_{Cl} in the l_{th} module. Fig.1 shows the hierarchical neural network of "neocognitron". In HTNSL, the layer of "C-cells" and "S-cells" are modelled as Layer type with names UUC and UUS respectively.

In a layer, either the S-cell or the C-cell will be divided into subgroups according to the optimal stimulus features of their respective fields. The cells in each subgroup are set in a two-dimensional array, which are modelled as Block type with names UC and US respectively corresponding to the C-cell and S-cell subgroupings.

As pointed out earlier that in a neural network some patterns of connection among a set of neurons exist repeatedly throughout the whole network. In "neocognitron" there are two patterns which exist between layers UUC and UUS to be called CSET and SSET respectively. The CSET is a pattern of connection from UUC to UUS, and SSET is a pattern of connection from

UUS to UUC. Fig.2 shows a pattern of connection of CSET where V is the inhibitory cell, $a(v)$ and b is modifiable by learning.

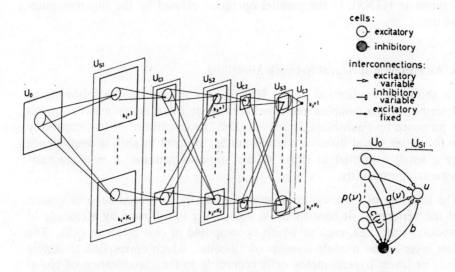

Fig.1 Schematic Diagram of Neocognotron.   Fig.2 C-cell Pattern.

The following formulae for computing the excitatory outputs(u_{Sl} and u_{Cl}) and the inhibitory outputs(v_{Cl-1} and v_{Sl}) of C-cells and S-cells are included in the **Method** of CSET, SSET, UUC and UUS respectively.

$$U_{Sl}(k_l,n) = r_l.\phi\left[\frac{1+\sum_{k_{l-1}=1}^{K_{l-1}}\sum_{v\in S_l} a_l(k_{l-1},v,k_l).U_{Cl-1}(k_{l-1},n+v)}{1+\frac{r_l}{1+r_1}b_l(k_l).v_{cl-1}(n)}-1\right]$$

$$U_{Cl}(k_l,n) = \psi\left[\frac{1+\sum_{v\in D_l} d_l(v).U_{Sl}(k_l,n+v)}{1+v_{Sl}(n)}-1\right]$$

$$v_{CI-1}(\mathbf{n}) = (\sum_{k_{I-1}=1}^{K_{I-1}} \sum_{v \in S_{sl}} c_{I-1}(v).U^2_{CI-1}(k_{I-1},\mathbf{n}+v))^{1/2}$$

$$v_{SI}(\mathbf{n}) = \frac{1}{K} \sum_{k=1}^{K_I} \sum_{v \in D_l} d_l(v).U_{SI}(k_l,\mathbf{n}+v)$$

where S_l and D_l are the domains covered by SSET and CSET respectively. The unmodifiable sypnases are $d_l(v)$ and $c_{l-1}(v)$ and the modifiable sypnases are $a_l(k_{l-1},v,k_l)$ and $b_l(k_l)$. For those neurons(denoted as n') which are highly activated as compared with their adjacent neurons the modifiable sypnases connected to them are modified by the following learning rules,

$$\Delta a_l(k_{l-1},v,k_l) = q_l.c_{l-1}(v).u_{Cl-1}(k_{l-1},n'+v),$$

$$\Delta b_l(k'_l) = q_l v_{Cl-1}(n')$$

In CSET and SSET the number of excitatory neurons are r*r and m*m respectively. There is only one inhibitory neuron in each of this pattern of connection, we did not explicitly name the inhibitory neuron as shown in the appendix listing of HTNSL code. However through the specifications in the Method of CSET and SSET written as: $VC(r*r |+wc)=sqrt(ec(i,j)*VC(i,j)**2)$ and

$VS(m*m |+wd)=wd(i.j)*VS(i,j)$ the output of the inhibitory neurons of CSET and SSET respectivly are defined.

UC and US are Block type having n*n instantiated copies of CSET and SSET with instantiated names CA[n*n] and SS[n*n] respectively. The input and output terminals of UC and US are made common to the respective terminals of CA[i,j] and SS[i,j]. Using Block type UC and US we produce Layer type UUC and UUS. Since in the UUC Layer type sypnases are modifiable by learning, thus a learning process is given in the Method of UUC. As the sypnases connection from UUS to UUC is not modifiable thus a similar Method is not there.

Finally 4 copies of UUC and 3 copies of UUS of Layer type are instantiated in Network NW. These copies of UUC and UUS named NUUC[i] and NUUS[i] respectively consist of different parameters to dimension its internal structures and initial values to initialize the network. They are read into the system by the Read statement in the Method of NW. The $io-spec$ of NW is to specifies the input and output interfacing files to the NW.

5. Conclusion

We have described a language for coding neural network. The modular features of this language would help the user to handle the complexity of a complicated neural network model. The design of this language which explore various possibilities of parallelism in PDP, should be suitable for implementation in supercomputers.

References

[1] D.E.Rumelhart and J.L.McClelland, Parallel Distribute Processing Vol.1 and Vol.2, MIT Press(1987).

[2] Willie Y.P.Lim, HISDL--A Structure Description Langauge, CACM Vol.25, No.11, 1982.

[3] K.Fukushima and Sei Miyake, Neocognitron, Pattern Recognition Vol.15 No.6, pp.455-462, 1982.

[4] D.H.Hubel and T.N.Wiesel, Receptive Fields, binocular interaction and functional architecture in cat's visual cortex. J.Physiol.(London) 160,106-154(1962).

Appendix

The following code of HTNSL specifies the model of Neocognitron and its learnig process.

```
Structure
PC(NW,UUC,UC,CSET)
PS(NW,UUS,US,SSET)
Endstructure


Pattern CSET(r >AC(r*r) <BC(r*r|+wa), VC(r*r|+wc|wb)
   Method
      BC(r*r|+wa) = wa(i,j)*BC(i,j)
      VC(r*r|+wc) = sqrt(wc(i,j)*VC(i,j)**2)
      VC(r*r|+wc|wb) = wb*VC(r*r|+wc)
   Endmethod
Endpattern

Pattern SSET(m >AS(m*m), BS(m*m) <VS(m*m|+wd))
   Method
      VS(m*m|+wd) = wd(i,j)*VS(i,j)
   Endmethod
Endpattern


Block UC(n,rc >IB(n*n) <OUK(n*n|wa), IV(n*n|wc)
   Instance CA[n*n]:CSET

   Connect
      For i=1,n ; j=1,n
      CA[i,j](rc >IB[i,j] <OUK[i,j], IV[i,j])
      Endfor
   Endconnect
Endblock


Block US(n,ms >IC(n*n), ID(n*n) <IV(n*n|wd))
   Instance SS[n*n]:SSET
   Connect
      For i=1,n; j=1,n
      SS[i,j](ms >IC[i,j] <ID[i,j], IV[i,j])
      Endfor
   Endconnect
Endblock
```

```
Layer UUC(ql,k,n1,r1 >IUC(k) <OVC(k|wa), OUC(k|wc|wb)

Instance UCI[k]:UC
         PC(t,k,n1*n1,r1*r1)

Connect
  For i=1,k
   UCI[i](n1,r1 >IUC[i] <OVC[i], OUC[i])
   For j=1,k
    /OVC[i|wa] UUS.IAS[j]/
    /OUC[i|wc|wb] UUS.IBS[j]/
   Endfor
  Endfor
Endconnect

Method
%Compute the excited neuron output in UUC layer
  For i=1,k
   TIUC = TIUC + IUC(i)
  Endfor
  For i=1,k
   OVCT = (1+IUC(i))/(1+TIUC) - 1
   If OVST>0.0
    OVC(i) = OVCT ; OUC(i) = OVCT
   Else
    OVC = 0.0 ; OUC = 0.0
   Endif
  Endfor
%Find the maximum output in each Block
  For s = 1,k
   LAV(s) = 0.0 ; LAI(s) = 1 ; LAJ(s) = 1
  Endfor
  For i=1,n1; j=1,n1
   LAX(1,i,j) = OVC#PC(t,1,i,j,-)
   For s=2,k
    LAX(s,i,j) = max(OVC#PC(t,s,i,j,&))
    If LAX(s,i,j) > LAX(s-1,i,j)
    Then  LAXV = LAX(s,i,j); LAXK = s; LAXI = i; LAXJ = j
    Endif
    If LAXV > LAV(LAXK)
    Then LAV(LAXK)=1; LAI(LAXK)=LAXI; LAJ(LAXK)=LAXJ
    Endif
   Endfor
  Endfor
% Updating of Weight
wa#PC(t,&&,LAI(&&),LAJ(&&),&) = wa#PC(t,&&,LAI(&&),&) +
ql*wc#PC(t,&&,LAI(&&),LAJ(&&),&)*OVC#PC(t,&&,LAI(&&),LAJ(&&),&)*LAV(&&)
wb#PC(t,&,LAI(&),LAJ(&),-)=ql*wc#PC(t,&,LAI(&),LAJ(&),-)*LAV(&)
Endmethod

Endlayer
```

Layer UUS(rp ,k ,nl ,r1 >IAS(k) IBS(k) <OVS(k|wd))

Instance USI[k]:US

Connect
For
/OVS[k] UUC.IUC[k]/
Endfor
Endconnect

Method
For s=1,k
  OVST(s) = rp*(1+IAS(s))/((rp/(1+rp)*IBS(s)) - 1
  If OVST(s) > 0
  Then OVS(s) = OVST(s)
  Else OVS(s) = 0.0
  Endif
  Endfor
Endmethod

Endlayer

Network (>INC <OUC[4])

Instance NUUC[4]:UUC
         NUUS[3]:UUS
         PC(4,kn[p],nn[p]*nn[p],rn[p]*rn[p])
         PS(3,kn[p],nn[p]*nn[p],rn[p]*rn[p])

Connect
  NUUC[1](qn[1],kn[1],nn[1],rn[1] >INC <OVC[1] OUC[1])
  For p=1,3
  NUUS[p](pn[p],kn[p],nn[p],rn[p] >OVC[p], OUC[p] <OVS[p])
  NUUC[p+1](qn[p+1],kn[p+1],nn[p+1],rn[p+1] >OVS[p] <OVC[p+1],OUC[p+1])
  Endfor
Endconnect

Method
%Initialization
For p=1,4
  Read qn[p],kn[p],nn[p],rn[p].
   wa#PC(p,&,&&,&&&,-)=FUN(p,&,&&,&&&,-)
   wb#PC(p,&,&&,&&&) = 0.0
  Read wc#PC(p,&,&&,&&&)
  Endfor
For p= 1,3
  Read wd#PS(p,&,&&,&&&,-)
  Endfor
Display wa#PC(2,2,1,2,1,2):timechart
Display wa#PC(2,2,1,2,&):barchart

Endnetwork

Part 2
Supercomputer Application in Mathematics

Vectorization of Lewis-Payne Random Number Generation on HITAC
S810 and S820

Large Scale Nonlinear Optimization Using a Cyber 205 Supercomputer

Supercomputer Oriented Numerical Algorithms for Sparse Matrix Computation

Calculation of pi to the 33 Million Decimal Places as Benchmark and Heat Run
Tests (Abstract)

Performance of Supercomputer Versions of NUMPAC (Abstract)

VECTORIZATION OF LEWIS-PAYNE RANDOM NUMBER GENERATION ON HITAC S810 AND S820

Yoshio Oyanagi

Institute of Information Sciences, University of Tsukuba

Tsukuba, Ibaraki, 305 Japan

Abstract

Fast algorithms for generating large set of random numbers on vector processors like HITAC S810 or S820 are presented. The vectorization of the multiplicative congruential method as well as Lewis-Payne method is shown. By the former method uniform random number is generated in every 2.5 nano seconds on S820.

1 Monte Carlo Simulation

The numerical simulation is one of the most important applications of supercomputers. It traces numerically a system which cosists of large number of 'elements' obeying a certain microscopic law of motion and the global behavior of the system is 'measured' numerically. The simulation is a method to predict macroscopic phenomena in terms of microscopic laws of motion.

If the system is deterministic, it can be simulated by a time integration of a certain differential equations. Such examples are in fluid dynamnics, meteorology, galaxy, plasma, semiconductor device, molecular dynamics, etc. On the other hand, if the system is stochastic, *i.e.* the basic equation of motion is defined by a stochastic process, we have to simulate "random" phenomena on a computer. It is called Monte Carlo simulation. Typical examples are neutron transfer, reactor simulation, magnetic materials, spin motion, thermodynamic simulation and QCD (quantum chromodynamics). In Monte Carlo simulations a huge set of random numbers, say, 10^{11} or more are used.

2 Multiplicative Congruential Method

The most popular method to generate pseudorandom numbers on digital computers is the linear congruential method[1]. Let x_i be a sequence of 32 bit odd integers, generated by

$$x_{i+1} = \lambda x_i \quad (\text{mod } 2^{31}). \tag{1}$$

This sequence x_i can be considered random provided $\lambda \equiv 3$ or 5 (mod 8). The period is 2^{29}. The usual uniform random number between 0 and 1 can be obtained by multiplying x_i by 2^{-31}.

The recurrence relation in Eq. 1 can be removed by using the associativity in multiplication in modulo,

$$x_{i+p} = \lambda^p x_i \quad (\text{mod } 2^{31}). \tag{2}$$

We give here a sample program.

```
        INTEGER LAM(N)
        REAL*8 X, F
        DATA MASK/Z7FFFFFFF/, F/Z3920000000000000/
        ..........
*  Initialization
        LAM(I)=48828125
        DO 10 I=2,N
   10   LAM(I)=LAM(I-1)*48828125
        ISEED=.......
        ..........
        DO 90 .....
        .......
          DO 20 I=1,N
             IX=LAM(I)*ISEED
             X =F*IAND(IX, MASK)
*  here X is used as a random number
        ..........
   20     CONTINUE
          ISEED=IX
        .......
   90   CONTINUE
```

Here LAM(I) stands for λ^I. We measured the performance of this program. For N=100000, it takes 2.5 m sec on S810/10 at KEK and 256 μ sec on S820/20 at University of Tokyo. Since the period is only $2^{29} \approx 5 \times 10^8$, the S820 can produce the whole period in 1.3 sec.

Moreover, the linear congruential random numbers have a lattice structure. As pointed by Marsaglia[2]), if the consecutive k random numbers are used to plot points in a k-dimensional hypercube, they lie in a relatively small number of $k-1$-dimensional parallel hyperplanes. We need better algorithm for large scale Monte Carlo simulation.

3　Lewis-Payne Method

Lewis and Payne[3] proposed a method to generate an integer sequence formed by

$$x_i = x_{i-p} \oplus x_{i-q}, \tag{3}$$

where $\oplus$ stands for the bitwise exclusive OR operator. The integer parameter p and q should be chosen so that the characteristic polynomial

$$f(D) = 1 + D^q + D^p \tag{4}$$

be primitive over the Galois field $GF(2)$. The period of this sequence is $2^p - 1$. Possible pairs of p and q are given in the following table. The pairs with p and $p - q$ are also acceptable.

p	q
31	3, 6, 7, 13
89	38
127	1, 7, 15, 30, 63
521	32, 48, 158, 168
607	105, 147, 273

In order to generate the sequence $\{x_i\}$, we must prepare the p initial values $x_1, \ldots, x_p$. The choice of the initial values is very crucial to the multidimensional uniformity as a random number sequence.

Fushimi and Tezuka[4] proposed the following initialization procedure, which garantees the k-distribution[5](uniformity in k-dimensional hypercube) for $k < p/32$.

Let $\{y_i\}$ be a 1-bit sequence generated by

$$y_i = y_{i-p} \oplus y_{i-q}. \tag{5}$$

The first p-bits $(y_1, \ldots, y_p)$ are arbitrary (excepts $y_i \equiv 0$) and may be generated by a linear congruential method. Fushimi and Tezuka proposed to generate $\{x_i\}$ in terms of the consecutive 32 bits in $\{y_i\}$, such as

$$
\begin{aligned}
x_1 &= & y_1 & \cdots & y_{32} \\
x_2 &= & y_{33} & \cdots & y_{64} \\
& & \cdots & & \\
x_p &= & y_{32p-31} & \cdots & y_{32p}
\end{aligned}
$$

The procedure has another advantage. The value of the autocorrelation over the whole period is almost zero up to phase difference $\tau \le (2^p - 1)/32$.

4 Vectorization

How can the generation of Lewis-Payne random number be vectorized? The trick in Eq. 2 can not be applicable in this case. We have, therefore, to vectorize Eq. 3 directly. To obtain high performance the vector should be as long as possible. The vector length is naturally limited by q due to the recurrence nature of Eq. 3, since x_{i-q} is referred to in calculating x_i. If $2q < p$, we should use $p - q$ in place of q.

There is other constraint on the vector length due to a buffer size effect. The integers $\{x_i\}$ are usually stored in a buffer with finite size. If the size is m, x_i is stored in IX(J) with $J = i \pmod{m}$. Whenever i or $i - p$ or $i - q$ pass an integer multiple of m, there should be a break of DO loop. In such a case the vector length is $p - q$, $m - p$, $m - p - q$, etc.

The minimum choise is $m = p$. In this case, Eq. 3 can be implemented as two DO loops with length q and $p - q$, provided $p - q > q$. The second minimum choice would be $m = p + q$. In this choice, the vector lengths are q, $p - q$ and q.

According to the preliminary experiment, it took 3.7 m sec on S810/10 and 620 μ sec on S820/80 to generate 100,000 uniform random numbers by this algorithm. It took only twice more CPU time as compared with the multiplicative congruential method as described in Section 2. We used $p = 607, q = 434$ and $m = p + q$.

Acknowledgement

Part of this work was done when the author stayed at National University of Singapore. He thanks Professor C. K. Yuen and his colleague for their warm hospitality.

References

[1] Lehmer, D. H., 'Mathematical Methods in Large-scale Computing Units,' *Proc. Second Symposium on Large-scale Digital Calculating Machinery* (Harvard University Press, Cambridge, Mass., 1951, pp. 141-146)

[2] Marsaglia, G., 'Random numbers fall mainly on the planes,' *Proc. Nat. Acad. Sci.* 61, 25-28 (1968).

[3] Lewis, T. G. and Payne, W. H., 'Generalized feedback shift-register pseudorandom number algorithms,' *J. of ACM* 21, 517-526 (1973).

[4] Fushimi, M., and Tezuka, S., 'Generation of pseudorandom numbers with uniform multidimensional distribution' *Japanese J. Applied Statistics* 10, 151-163 (1982).

[5] Knuth, D. E., *The Art of Computer Programming* Vol. 2:*Seminumerical Algorithms.* 2nd Ed. (Addison-Wesley, Reading, Mass., 1981)

LARGE SCALE NONLINEAR OPTIMIZATION USING
A CYBER 205 SUPERCOMPUTER

Dr Phua Kang Hoh, Paul
Department of Information Systems and Computer Science
National University of Singapore
SINGAPORE

ABSTRACT

Vectorization of the nonlinear conjugate-gradient method applied to solve large scale unconstrained minimization problems on a CYBER 205 supercomputer has been investigated in this paper. Using the timing routines (SPY) of the CYBER 205 it became evident that for large scale meteorological minimization problems considered, the function and gradient evaluation routines dominate the CPU time spent in the total minimization process. By performing automatic and then manual vectorization, we succeeded in achieving a sizable reduction in the CPU time required for finding the local minimum of nonlinear functions of 10^4 -- 10^5 variables. This shows that vector computers are advantageous in the case of large scale nonlinear optimizations.

1. INTRODUCTION

The optimization problem with which this paper is concerned is to find a local minimizer $\underline{x}^*$ of a nonlinear real-valued function $f(\underline{x})$, where

$$\underline{x} = (x_1, x_2, \ldots, x_n)^T , \quad n \geq 1$$

can be any real numbers. By large-scale numerical optimization, we will mean the minimization of functions where n, the number of variables, is large. Typically, the value of n can be up to the order of 100,000 variables.

All numerical techniques for unconstrained optimization are iterative, starting with an initial estimate $\underline{x}_0$ to $\underline{x}^*$ and proceeding to generate a sequence of estimates to the minimizer by:

$$\underline{x}_{k+1} = \underline{x}_k + \alpha_k \, \underline{d}_k \tag{1.1}$$

where $\underline{d}_k$ is an appropriately chosen search vector, and α_k is the step-length scalar.

52

Classically, the oldest and simplest known search technique is the steepest descent method. Here the sequence (1.1) becomes

$$\underline{x}_{k+1} = \underline{x}_k - \alpha_k g_k \ , \tag{1.2}$$

where $g_k = \nabla f(\underline{x}_k)$, is the gradient of f evaluated at $\underline{x}_k$. It can be shown that this method converges from an arbitiary starting point to a local stationary point of f with a proper choice of α_k. Further, it can be shown that at each point of the sequence

$$f(\underline{x}_{k+1}) < f(\underline{x}_k), \tag{1.3}$$

and thus the stationary point is likely to be a local minimizer.

The difficulty with the steepest descent method lies in the rate of convergence of the sequence (1.2). It can be shown that for $f(\underline{x})$ a quadratic function, the sequence has a linear rate of convergence with a constant rate of

$$\rho = \frac{\lambda \text{max} - \lambda \text{min}}{\lambda \text{max} + \lambda \text{min}} \ , \tag{1.4}$$

where λmax and λmin are the largest and smallest eigenvalues of the Hessian matrix of f. Thus for problems with ill-conditioned Hessians, convergence can be extremely slow even for simple quadratic objective function.

Another classical method, Newton's method, solves quadratic minimization problems in a single step. Here the sequence (1.1) becomes

$$\underline{x}_{k+1} = \underline{x}_k - J_k^{-1} g_k \ , \tag{1.5}$$

where J_k is the Hessian matrix of f evaluated at $\underline{x} = \underline{x}_k$. Additional advantages of Newton's Method are that for functions with bounded third derivatives and for $\underline{x}_0$ sufficiently close to $\underline{x}^*$, the method converges with a quadratic rate of convergence, that is,

$$\| \underline{x}_{k+1} - \underline{x}^* \|^2 \leq K \ \| \underline{x}_k - \underline{x}^* \|^2 \ , \tag{1.6}$$

where K is an asymptotic constant.

A major difficulty with Newton's method is that second derivatives of the objective function must be calculated, which may be computationally expensive. Furthermore, away from $\underline{x}^*$, J_k may well not be a positive definite matrix, leading to increasing, rather than decreasing values of $f(\underline{x})$. In fact, it can be **shown** that for convex functions, if $\underline{x}_0$ is sufficiently far from $\underline{x}^*$, the sequence (1.5) can diverge unless linear searches are introduced to find $\alpha_k < 1$ to reduce $f(\underline{x}_{k+1})$. For nonconvex objective functions, positive α_k which reduces $f(\underline{x})$ may not exist. Finally, for problems with a large number of variables, the matrix J_k may require excessive storage, which can also make the solution of the system of linear equations

$$J_k \, \underline{d}_k = -\underline{g}_k \, , \qquad\qquad (1.7)$$

very costly, even if J_k can be stored.

Section 2 of the paper deals with conjugate gradient methods which are found to be suitable for solving large-scale optimization problems. Their relationship to the quasi-Newton method will also be discussed.

In Section 3, we shall describe two relevant large scale meteorological problems where the constrained nonlinear optimization was applied. We shall show that how these two constrained problems can be transformed into a form of large-scale unconstrained optimization problems.

In their paper, Navon and Legler [9] discovered that the nonlinear optimization software package developed by Shanno and Phua [17] is the most consistent and performing one currently available for solving their large-scale meteorological problems. Special features and characteristics of this piece of software will be discussed in Section 4.

The vectorization of conjugate gradient methods will be discussed in Section 5. The vectorization of the function and gradient evaluations of the above two problems will also be discussed. Further, outlines on the architectures of the vector supercomputer CYBER 205 will also be discussed in this Section.

Finally, results concerning the performance of a particular conjugate-gradient code under scalar, automatic vectorization and refined manual vectorization are summarized in Section 6 with conclusion remarks.

2. NUMERICAL TECHNIQUES FOR SOLVING LARGE-SCALE OPTIMIZATION

Different numerical algorithms are available (see for instance Gill et al. [4]) for solving large-scale optimization problems. On one hand we have simple techniques such as the steepest descent method which converges linearly, while on the other hand we have Newton and Quasi-Newton methods which have quadratic rates of convergence and superlinear rates of convergence respectively but require storage of Hessian matrices of second derivatives of size (nxn).

The algorithms that we are going to introduce now share a common salient point, that is, they all do not require the storage of Hessian matrices. These techniques can be implemented using storage of 3 to 7 vectors of length n, and have nice computational features for vector and parallel computers. With superlinear rates of convergence, conjugate gradient methods seem to be the only choice open for large-scale optimization problems.

Historically, conjugate gradient methods were developed by Hestenes and Stiefel [5] to solve systems of linear equations. The system

$$A\underline{x} = \underline{b} \qquad (2.1)$$

was solved by minimizing

$$Q(\underline{x}) = (A\underline{x} - \underline{b})^T(A\underline{x} - \underline{b}) \qquad (2.2)$$

which clearly has a minimum at a solution to (2.1). The method is iterative, starting with an initial estimate $\underline{x}_0$ to the minimizer and an initial search direction

$$\underline{d}_0 = -g_0 = -\nabla Q(\underline{x}_0)$$

and proceeding by

$$\underline{x}_{k+1} = \underline{x}_k + \alpha_k \underline{d}_k \qquad (2.3)$$

$$\underline{d}_{k+1} = -g_{k+1} + \beta_k \underline{d}_k \qquad (2.4)$$

where

$$\beta_k = \frac{g_{k+1}^T y_k}{y_k^T d_K} \qquad (2.5)$$

where $y_k = g_{k+1} - g_k$. It can be shown that with exact computer arithmetic, the sequence (2.3) - (2.5) minimized (2.2) in at most n steps providing α_k is chosen to minimize $Q(\underline{x})$ along d_k at each step. For **quadratic** objective functions, such as (2.2), it is possible to show that α_k satisfies

$$\beta_k = \frac{g_{k+1}^T \, g_{k+1}}{g_k^T \, g_k} \tag{2.6}$$

For general nonlinear objective functions $f(x)$, Fletcher and Reeves [3] generalized the conjugate gradient method simply by substituting $g(x) = \nabla f(x)$ for $g(x) = \nabla Q(x)$ in the above sequence. The Fletcher-Reeves code has β_k chosen by (2.6). Polak and Rebiere [12] showed that the equivalence of (2.5) and (2.6) depended both upon exact linear searches and $f(x)$ being quadratic. For non-quadratic $f(x)$, they suggested

$$\beta_k = \frac{g_{k+1}^T \, y_k}{g_k^T \, g_k} \quad, \tag{2.7}$$

which is equivalent to (2.5) for nonquadratic objective functions when exact linear searches are used. For inexact linear searches, which prevail in contemporary codes, (2.5) is the correct β_k to assure conjugacy.

Perry [11] noted that for β_k defined by (2.5), (2.4) can be rewritten as

$$d_{k+1} = -(I - \frac{d_k \, y_k^T}{y_k^T \, d_k}) \, g_{k+1} \tag{2.8}$$

and Shanno [15] showed that for exact linear searches, (2.8) is equivalent to

$$d_{k+1} = -(I - \frac{\delta_k \, y_k^T + y_k \delta_k^T}{\delta_k^T \, y_k} + (1 + \frac{y_k^T y_k}{\delta_k^T \, y_k}) \, \frac{\delta_k \delta_k^T}{\delta_k^T \delta_k}) \, g_{k+1}$$

$$\tag{2.9}$$

where $\delta_k = \alpha_k \, d_k$. But (2.9) is exactly the BFGS update formula of quasi-Newton methods with H_k replaced by the identity matrix I. Thus for inexact searches, d_{k+1} defined by (2.9) is a descent direction.

A difficulty with conjugate gradient methods is the rate of convergence. If every n iterations the search direction is reset to be $d_{k+1} = -g_{k+1}$, then is at best linear. Beale [1] suggested a restart procedure which preserves superlinear convergence, but never reset the

search direction to the negative gradient direction. He stores two additional vectors, and compute d_{k+1} by

$$d_{k+1} = -g_{k+1} + \beta_k \, d_k + r_k \, d_r \quad , \qquad (2.10)$$

where d_r is the restart vector, and y_r is also stored in order to compute r_k.

Shanno and Phua [16] showed that d_{k+1} defined in (2.10) can be computed as a double BFGS update of the form (2.9), and they have implemented a code which allows the user to choose either a conjugate gradient direction computed by (2.9) with Beale restarts, or a quasi-Newton method using the BFGS update formulas. The software uses the same linear search technique to determine α_k for both methods, with the additional condition that for the conjugate gradient method, at least two trial points be used at each iteration. Extensive computational experience with the code shows that for problems with a small number of variables, the quasi-Newton method is superior, but for a large number of variables, the conjugate gradient method is generally faster, and often substantially faster.

As a final note for this section, Powell [13] has shown that the Fletcher-Reeves [3] conjugate gradient method without restarts is globally convergent for general nonlinear objective functions, but all other conjugate methods discussed here may fail to converge by cycling through a fixed set of points bounded away from the minimizer. Shanno [15] showed that if we defined r_k by

$$r_k^2 = \frac{t}{\|g_k\|^2 \sum\limits_{i=1}^{k} \frac{1}{\|g_i\|^2}} \quad , \quad 0 < t < 1, \qquad (2.11)$$

and let

$$\theta_k^2 = \frac{(g_k^T d_k)^2}{\|g_k\|^2 \|d_k\|^2} \quad , \qquad (2.12)$$

then if d_k is reset to $-g_k$ whenever $\theta_k^2 \geq r_k^2$, all methods are globally convergent. Further, for badly nonlinear problems, with t in the range $0.05 \leq t \leq 0.2$, this restarting improves computational performance. Thus selective restarts should be done , but only under very restrictive conditions.

3. LARGE-SCALE METEOROLOGICAL PROBLEM

In this section, we introduce two large-scale meteorological problems where nonlinear optimization techniques were applied. These two problems are formulated as constrained minimization problems, but they are solved as a sequence of unconstrained minimization problems using conjugate gradient methods.

3.1. The Shallow-Water Equations

Here, we consider the shallow-water equation of enforcing simultaneous conservation of three integral invariants: the total mass, total energy and potential enstrophy, on a limited-area domain (see Navon [7]).

In our case, we define a functional f by

$$f = \sum_{j=1}^{Nx} \sum_{k=1}^{Ny} [\alpha(u-\bar{u})^2 + \alpha(\nu - \bar{\nu})^2 + \beta(h-\bar{h})^2]_{jk}^n, \qquad (3.1)$$

where $Nx \, \Delta x = L$, $Ny \, \Delta y = D$, $\Delta x = \Delta y = h$ is the grid size while n designates the time-level $t_n = n \, \Delta t$, where Δt is the time-step, while L and D are the respective dimensions of the rectangular domain over which the shallow-water equations are being solved (see Navon & de Villiers [8]).

Here, $(\bar{u},\bar{\nu},\bar{h})^n_{jk}$ are the predicted variables at the nth time step using a finite-difference algorithm, whereas $(u,\nu,h)^n_{jk}$ are the field values adjusted by the nonlinear constrained optimization method using the augmented-Lagrangian technique to enforce conservation of the three integral invariants of the shallow-water equation. Here α and β are the relative weights selected so as to make the fractional adjustments of variables proportional to the fractional magnitude of the truncation errors in the predicted variables. Indeed, we used

$$\alpha = 1 \qquad and \qquad \beta = g/H$$

where H is the mean depth of the shallow-fluid.

The augmented-Lagrangian function $\emptyset$ is defined by

$$\emptyset(\underline{x},\underline{\lambda},r) = f(\underline{x}) + \lambda^T e(\underline{x}) + \frac{1}{2r} |e(\underline{x})|^2 \qquad (3.2)$$

and the minimization of (3.2) replaces the following original constrained minimization problem:

$$\text{minimize } f(\underline{x}) \tag{3.3}$$

$$\text{subject to } e(\underline{x}) = 0, \quad e = (e_1, \ldots, e_n)^T, \quad m \leq n$$

where $e(\underline{x})$ are the equality constraints. Here

$$\underline{x} = (u_{11}, \ldots, u_{NxNy}, v_{11}, \ldots, v_{NxNy}, h_{11}, \ldots, h_{NxNy})^T$$

and in our particular case, the equality constraint vector has three components given by

$$e(\underline{x}) = \begin{cases} E^n - E^o \\ Z^n - Z^o \\ H^n - H^o \end{cases}$$

where

$$E^n = \frac{1}{2} \sum_{j=1}^{Nx} \sum_{k=1}^{Ny} [h(u^2+v^2)+gh^2]^n_{jk} \, \Delta x \Delta y$$

$$Z^n = \frac{1}{2} \sum_{j=1}^{Nx} \sum_{k=1}^{Ny} [(\frac{v}{x} - \frac{u}{y} + f)/h]^{2n}_{jk} \, \Delta x \Delta y$$

$$H^n = \sum_{j=1}^{Nx} \sum_{k=1}^{Ny} h_{jk} \, \Delta x \Delta y$$

Here, E^n, Z^n, and H^n are the discrete values of the integral invariants of the total energy, potential enstrophy and mass at time $t_n = n \Delta t$, whereas E^n, Z^n, and H^n are the discrete values of the integral invariants of the total energy, potential enstrophy and mass at time $t_n = n\Delta t$, whereas E^o, Z^o, and H^o are the values of the same integral invariants at the initial time $t=o$, $\underline{\lambda}$ is an m component Lagrangian multiplier vector and r is a penalty parameter.

In our application, we follow the augmented Lagrangian algorithm of Bertsekas [2] for minimizing the following function:

$$L_{rk}(\underline{x}, \underline{\lambda}_k) = f(\underline{x}) + \underline{\lambda}_k^T e(\underline{x}) + \frac{1}{2r_k} |e(\underline{x})|^2$$

and updating the Lagrange multipliers and penalty parameters. Here k is an index of the iteration sequence. For the inexact unconstrained minimization of the augmented-Lagrangian $L_{rk}(\underline{x}_k, \underline{\lambda}_k)$, we use a conjugate-gradient method which has the virtue of requiring only a few vectors for memory storage. This conjugate-gradient method will be described in details in the **next** Section.

For this application, we used two grids -- a coarse mesh grid with a space increment of

$$\Delta x = \Delta y = 400 \text{ km}, \quad \Delta t = 3600 \text{ sec}$$

where Δt is the time step. This resulted in a grid of 12 by 15 in the x and y directions respectively for a rectangular domain of L = 4400 km and D = 6000 km.

The augmented-Lagrangian function was a function of $\underline{x}$ which had 12x15x3 = 540 variables. A second grid using a refined mesh space increment of

$$\Delta x = \Delta y = 40 \text{ km}, \quad \Delta t = 360 \text{ sec}$$

was also tested resulting in 150 x 111 x 3 $\simeq$ 50,000 variables in the nonlinear unconstrained minimization.

3.2 The Problem of Suppressing Lamb Waves

In meteorological applications, one is often interested in suppressing external gravity waves by modifying the observed wind field in such a way that the vertical motions at the lowest level of a 3-dimensional atmospheric model vanish. An alternative way is to regard this adjustment as a variational adjustment of the horizontal wind fields in a pressure coordinate system (x,y,p) so that the pressure tendency dp_s/dt is zero everywhere. Here p_s is the surface pressure.

The continuity equation in pressure coordinate is given by

$$\frac{\partial u}{\partial x} - \frac{\partial v}{\partial y} - \frac{\partial w}{\partial p} = 0$$

Integrating this equation from the top to the bottom of the atmosphere and assuming the vertical velocity w=0 at both end points, we obtain (see [10])

$$\int_0^{Ps} \left(\frac{\partial u}{\partial x} + \frac{\partial v}{\partial y} \right) dp = 0$$

Using this equation as a constraint will ensure that

$$\frac{dPs}{dt} = 0$$

In other words, using the continuity equation as a strong constraint will enable us to suppress Lamb waves (see [10]).

The Lamb waves are high speed acoustic-gravity waves which appear as solutions to the primitive equations in numerical weather prediction along with slow, physically relevant meteorological waves. As such, we are interested in suppressing the Lamb waves which can be viewed as noise in a meteorological model and which impose very stringent computational stability conditions on the allowable time step Δt.

The functional for which the stationary value is to be found for this problem is:

$$f = \int_x \int_y \int_p [(u-\bar{u})^2 + (v-\bar{v})^2] dx\,dy\,dp$$
$$+ \int_x \int_y [\lambda \int_0^{P_s} (\frac{\partial u}{\partial x} + \frac{\partial v}{\partial y}) dp] dx\,dy$$

where $\bar{u}$ and $\bar{v}$ are the analyzed horizontal wind components, while u and v are the observed horizontal wind components, and λ is the Lagrange multiplier.

In a discrete augmented-Lagrangian formulation, we have:

$$\emptyset = \sum_i \sum_j \sum_k [(U_{ijk} - U_{ijk})^2 + (V_{ijk} - V_{ijk})^2] \Delta x \Delta y \Delta p$$

$$+ \sum \sum_k \lambda_{ij} [\sum_k (\frac{U_{i+1,jk} - U_{i-1,j,k}}{2\Delta x})$$

$$+ \frac{V_{i,j+1,k} - V_{i,j-1,k}}{2\Delta y}) \Delta p] \Delta x \Delta y$$

$$+ \frac{1}{2} \sum_i \sum_j C_{ij} [\sum_k (\frac{U_{i+1,j,k} - U_{i-1,j,k}}{2\Delta x})$$

$$+ \frac{V_{i,j+1,k} - V_{i,j-1,k}}{2\Delta y}) \Delta p]^2 \Delta x \Delta y$$

where C_{ij} are the penalty parameters,
and λ_{ij} are the Lagrange multipliers.

Our model domain is rectangular while in the vertical we have 10 discrete levels resulting in the application in a function 23x23x10x2 components, i.e. 10580 components. A finer mesh case where the mesh spacing was increased by a factor of 2 in the horizontal resulted in a function of 46x46x10x2 components, i.e. 42320 variables. Here the vector of variables $\underline{x}$ is given by:

$$\underline{x} = (U_{111}, \ldots, U_{N_xN_yN_p}, V_{111}, \ldots, V_{N_xN_yN_p})^T$$

for the three dimensional limited-area domain in x,y, and $P(N_x\Delta x=L, N_y\Delta y=D, N_p\Delta p=H)$.

The gradient of the discrete augmented-Lagrangian function $\emptyset$ with respect to $\underline{x}$ is given by:

$$\left.\frac{\partial\emptyset}{\partial U}\right|_{ijk} = 2(U_{ijk} - U_{ijk})\Delta_x\Delta_y\Delta_p$$

$$+ \left(\frac{\lambda_{i-j,j} - \lambda_{i+1,j}}{2\Delta x}\right) \Delta x\Delta y\Delta p$$

$$+ \sum_k \left(\frac{U_{i+1,j,k} - U_{i-1,j,k}}{2\Delta x} + \frac{V_{i,j+1,k} - V_{i,j-1,k}}{2\Delta y}\right)$$

$$\Delta p. \left(\frac{C_{i-1,j} - C_{i+1,j}}{2\Delta x}\right) \Delta x\Delta y$$

$$\left.\frac{\partial\emptyset}{\partial V}\right|_{ijk} = 2(V_{ijk} - V_{ijk}) \Delta x\Delta y\Delta p$$

$$+ \frac{\lambda_{i,j-1} - \lambda_{i,j+1}}{2\Delta y} \Delta x\Delta y\Delta p$$

$$+ \sum_k \left(\frac{U_{i+1,j,k} - U_{i-1,j,k}}{2\Delta x} + \frac{V_{i,j+1,k} V_{i,j-1,k}}{2\Delta y}\right)$$

$$\Delta p. \left(\frac{C_{i,j-1} - C_{i,j+1}}{2\Delta y}\right) \cdot \Delta x\Delta y$$

The same inexact minimization of the augmented-Lagragian of Bertsekas [2] is applied using the same rules for updating the Lagrange multipliers and the penalty parameters.

4. THE SHANNO-PHUA OPTIMIZATION SOFTWARE

In their paper, Navon and Legler [9] studied the practical performances of four conjugate-gradient codes, namely Fletcher-Rerves [3], Polak-Ribiere [12], Powell's restart method [13], and Shanno-Phua's [17] quasi-Newton memoryless method. These four representative up-to-date available scientific software were applied to solve various large-scale meteorological problems, using criteria of computational economy and accuracy. From the conjugate-gradient methods that they have tested, they found that the most consistent and performing one for most applications turned out to the Shanno-Phua [17] quasi-Newton memoryless conjugate-gradient algorithm.

The CONMIN software package developed by Shanno and Phua [17] finds a local minimizes of a nonlinear objective function of n variables, $f(\underline{x})$, where

$$\underline{x} = (x_1, x_2, \ldots, x_n)^T, \quad n \geq 1$$

can be any real numbers. This software package incorporates two nonlinear optimization techniques, i.e. a conjugate-gradient algorithm and a quasi-Newton algorithm, with the choice of the method left to the user. The quasi-Newton method is the BFGS algorithm with initial scaling documented in Shanno and Phua [16]. This method requires approximately $1n^2/2 + 11^n/2$ single or double precisions words of working storage.

The conjugate-gradient algorithm in CONMIN is the Beale restarted memoryless variable metric algorithm documented in Shanno [15]. This method requires approximately $7n$ single/double precision words of working space to be provided by the user. For solving large-scale nonlinear optimization problems, memory considerations generally mandate using the conjugate-gradient algorithm.

The CONMIN subroutine was modified so as to maximize the vectorization of its code on the CYBER 205 supercomputers. Some special features and characteristics of CDC supercomputers will be discussed in the next Section. As will be shown in Section 6, the performance of this conjugate-gradient code can be significantly improved by careful implementation on super-computers when solving large-scale nonlinear optimization problems. The detailed algorithmic description of the modified Shanno-Phua [17] conjugate-gradient is given in [10], we summarize here the main steps of this algorithm as follows:

(1) Initialization

Choose $\underline{x}_0$, ε, $H_0 = I$ and set $k=0$,
Compute: $\underline{s}_k = - \nabla f(\underline{x}_k)$

(2) Perform the inexact linear search procedure proposed by Shanno & Phua [16] to find α_k such that

$$f(\underline{x}_k + \alpha_k \underline{s}_k) < f(\underline{x}_k)$$

(3) Compute the new estimate:

$$\underline{x}_{k+1} = \underline{x}_k + \alpha_k \underline{s}_k$$

(4) If the convergence criterion is satisfied, then stop; else proceed to step (5).

(5) If the restart criterion proposed by Powell [13] holds, then perform the Beale [1] restart procedure and repeat from step (2) ; else proceed to step (6).

(6) Compute the new search direction by the two-step memoryless BFGS formula proposed by Shanno-Phua [17] and repeat from step (2).

For the above description, it is evident that there are two distinct types of iteration in the modified CONMIN subroutine, namely a restart iteration and a normal (non-restart) iteration. Each restart iteration involves the execution of steps (2)-(5) whereas a normal iteration consists of steps (2),(3),(4), and (6). In their paper, Navon, Phua and Raramurthy [10] analysed the computational complexity of the modified CONMIN routine in terms of the number of operations (multiplications and additions) required per each iteration. They have shown that the amount operations in performing a restart iteration of the modified CONMIN routine is at most 11n multiplications and additions, whereas it requires 21n additions and 23n multiplications to perform a normal iteration. As for the question on how frequent a restart iteration is performed in comparison to a normal iteration, computational experiences showed that in general, a restart was being made every two to three iterations. It was extremely rare for a given direction to be used for more than ten iterations. Working on the assumption that every third iteration of the modified CONMIN subroutine is a restart iteration, it can be shown that the average number of additions and multiplications required per each iteration of this code are 18.5n and 20n respectively.

The basic formula for CPU time consumption in an optimization code is (see [10]):

$$T = t_f n_f + t_g n_g + t_i n_i$$

where t_f and t_g are the CPU times required per each function and gradient calculation respectively, while t_i is the average overhead execution time per iteration. Here n_f is the number of function evaluations, n_g is the number of gradient evaluations, and n_i is the number of iterations. The computational effort of function and gradient evaluation is problem dependent but as a rule, it becomes the most expensive part of the whole optimization process as the number of variables increases, ie. for large-scale optimization problems.

The computational complexity of the test problems described in Section 2 will be further discussed in Section 6.

5. VECTORIZATION TECHNIQUES

Amongst the major developments in recent years in the field of computing, one should attribute the introduction of a variety of vector and parallel computers and the development of appropriate algorithms to efficiently utilize their capabilities.

For nonlinear conjugate-gradient methods, a thorogh review of the available literature shows the fact that the research activity carried by a small number of researchers was directed towards efforts in paralleliz- ing the methods, and to our best knowledge, no effort was directed toward vectorizing the methods. Paral- lelization of the nonlinear conjugate-gradient method can be introduced by approximating the successive gradients by finite-differences of the function values calculated in parallel, and one can also accelerate the linear searches by simultaneous function evaluations at preselected gridpoints along the search direction. For instance, Schandel [14] designed parallel version of Powell's direct search technique generating conjugate search directions by minimization over geometrically parallel manifolds. This results in simultaneous linear searches but computational experience up to date is too limited, see Lootsma [6].

No report appears to be available of **speeding up**
the nonlinear conjugate-gradient methods for large scale
optimization on vector computers. This issue is of
crucial importance when we solve problems with expensive
function/gradient evaluations. It is important to
develop efficient unconstrained optimization algorithms
not only because the problem occurs in many instances on
its own, but even more so because an unconstrined
optimization problem must be solved in the inner-loop of
the solution of many constrained optimization problems.
As mentioned by Schandel [14], vector computers can be
advantageous in case of large-scale unconstrained
optimization.

In this section, we describe various steps taken to
speed-up the performance of the modified CONMIN algorithm for the CYBER 205 vector computer. This
supercomputer has 4 million 64-bit words of central
memory, two vector pipelines, 20 ns clock, and approximately 7 gigabytes of disk storage. Because of its
memory-to-memory architecture, the CYBER 205 has a
longer vector start-up time than, say, a register-to-
register supercomputer such as a CRAY X-MP, see Figure
1. In order to achieve top performance, it becomes
necessary to increase the vector length on the CYBER 205
to fairly long vectors. For the CYBER 205, the half-
performance length is about 100, whereas on the CRAY X-
MP it is around 10 elements. The half-performance
length can be defined as the vector length needed to
achieve one-half the asymptotic peak vector operation
rate.

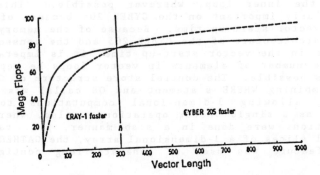

Figure 1. Performance of the 2-pipe CYBER 205 (broken
line) and the CRAY-1 (full line) as a function
of vector length.

Source : Hockney and Jesshope, Parallel Computers:
Architecture, Programming and Algorithms,1981.

Since the CYBER 205 is a memory-to-memory vector pipeline machine, this means that it calculates a string (vector) of identical operations on adjacently positioned memory locations, producing between 2 and 0.2 results/clock cycle/vector pipe. The machine can be configured with up to 4 vector pipes. Unlike the majority of vector pipeline and array processor machines, CDC/ETA machines run a FORTRAN compiler with explicit vector extensions. Consequently a user has the option of either using the vector optimizing compiler or he can choose to code the vector instructions explicity.

To exploit the full potential of supercomputers, algorithms must be developed and codes designed with the specific machine architecture in mind. The gap between hardware and software must be constantly bridged to make effective use of the capabilities of these systems. We shall now describe the steps taken to speed up and to optimize the performance of CYBER 205 for solving the meterological problems described in Section 3.

One of the first steps in vectorizing any codes is to determine where the supercomputer spends the bulk of its execution time. A flow analysis (e.g. SPY on the CYBER 205) provides this information, enabling us to isolate and concentrate on these sections of the code that consumes the largest fractions of the time.

The second step in vectorizing is to restructure the code such that the loop with the largest range became the inner loop, wherever possible. This is particularly important on the CYBER 205 because of its longer vector start-up time. Because of the memory-to-memory architecture of the CYBER 205 and the consequent increase in the vector start-up time, it is imperative that the number of elements in vector loops be kept as large as possible. The control store structure of CYBER 205 (combining WHERE statement and Q8 calls) was very useful, allowing 3-dimensional computations to be treated as a single vector operations. Also, wherever computations were done in a slab manner, i.e. taking vectical slices of a 3-dimensional array, the GATHER/SCATTER feature was used to generate long contiguous vectors.

Other vectorization techniques that were implemented include: removing dependencies by re-ordering DO loops, isolating recursive portions of loops, and collecting intermediate results in temporary vectors to increase the number of vectorizable loops and to make optimum use of triadic operations.

The conjugate-gradient algorithm involves two principal components of code that consume most of the CPU time:

1) The actual minimization procedure
2) The function and gradient evaluation

As a first step, the minimization routine, CONMIN, was restructured so that all DO-loops could be vectorized. The bulk of the DO-loops in this procedure were used to perform inner product and summation operations. On the CYBER 205, these operations are initiated by a certain type of machine instructions called vector macros. Although both of the computations are reduction operations, they are vectorizable because of their hardware implementation.

The floating point 'add' and 'multiply' units on the CYBER 205 have feed back connections for accumulative addition and multiplication operations. Further, the result from any of the functional units can be routed directly to the input of other units without stopping in some intermediate registers, or referencing of memory. This process, known as 'short stopping', gives an effective stream rate of one result per cycle. The timing information for summation and innter product operations are as follows:

Operation	Timing
Q8 SSUM	96 + N cycles
Q8 SDOT	107 + N cycles

After the initial vector start-up time of 96 and 107 cycles for 'Add' and 'multiply' respectively, a new result becomes available after each cycle. Therefore, the larger the N, the lesser the impact of the start-up time on the final performance of the two operations.

Having vectorized the minimization routine, the next task is to vectorize the FUNCT routine, which calculates the values of the objective function and its corresponding gradient for subsequent use in CONMIN. We have applied the CONMIN routine to two separate meteorological problems (see Section 3). However, for the sake of brevity, we shall only describe the vectorization techniques used for the Lamb wave problem only.

The Lamb wave problem is a multi-dimensional boundary value problem, and the minimization is done only in the interior of the domain. In order to achieve top performance on the CYBER 205, the two- and three-dimensional arrays are collapsed into one-dimensional arrays. The computation of the objective function and its gradient can be vectorized over all three dimensions

by collapsing the DO loops in the three spatial directions into an one-dimensional DO loop and making use of
the control bit vectors. Such collapsing operation can
be done very efficiently in a bit addressable supercomputer such as CYBER 205 with the help of WHERE statement. WHERE statements enable us to mask the results
along the boundary grid points by pre-initializing these
addresses to zero bits with Q8VMKO calls. Also, the
largest loop range was made the inner-most loop wherever
possible.

6. COMPUTATIONAL RESULTS AND DISCUSSIONS

The nonlinear optimization software package, CONMIN
(see Section 4), proposed by Shanno and Phua [17] was
applied to solve two meteorological problems, namely,
the Shallow-Water equations and the Lamb wave problem
described in Section 3. The CONMIN routine was modified
so that all the DO-loops were readily vectorized by the
automatic vectorizing FORTRAN compiler of the CYBER 205.

By running the vectorized version of CONMIN
routine, it became evident that the bulk of CPU time was
spent in the function and gradient evaluation procedure
for these two problems. This is particularly true when
the dimensions of two problems were increased. As such
our vectorization effort was also directed towards the
performance improvements of the function and gradient
evaluation routines.

As a starting point of this effort, we began with
the automatic vectorization of the function and gradient
routines by using the FORTRAN compiler. This process is
referred as "automatic vectorization" in this paper.
Further improvement in the speed-up of performance was
achieved by using various vectorization techniques
mentioned in Section 5 to restructure the FUNCT routines. This process is hereby referred as "supervectorization" or "manual vectorization".

For the first test problem namely, the Shallow-
Water equations, the results obtained by using scalar
computations, vector computations with automatic
vectorization and supervectorization are summarized in
Table I.

Table I.   Computational Results for the Shallow-**Water**
            Equations

Mesh/	CPU Time (secs)		
Dimension	Scalar	Automatic Vectorization	Super-Vectorization
12x15x3 =540	0.01238	0.01128	0.00722
150x111x3 ≈50,000	1.17728	0.93970	0.17398

The speed-up ratio was computed by taking the ratio of
the CPU time obtained by scalar computations versus the
CPU time obtained by vector computations respectively.
These results are presented in Table II.   For this
problem, the speed-up due to vectorization was a factor
of about 7 for the fine mesh case (111 x 150). For a
very corase mesh version (12 x 15) of this problem, the
speed-up due to vectorization was only by a factor of
less than 2, this reflects the longer start-up time for
vector computations on the CYBER 205 supercomputer.

Table II. Speed-up Ratios for The Shallow-Water
           Equations

Mesh/	Speed-up Ratio		
Dimension	Scalar Computations	Automatic Vectorization	Super-Vectorization
12x15x3 =540	1	1.10	1.71
150x111x3 ~50,000	1	1.25	6.73

     As for the second test problems namely, the Lamb
wave problem, the similar computational results are
summarized in Tables III & IV.

Table III. Computational Results for the Lamb wave problem

Mesh/	CPU Time (secs)		
Dimension	Scalar Computations	Automatic Vectorization	Super-Vectorization
23x23x10x2 = 10.580	3.2494	1.8126	0.2015
46x46x10x2 = 42.320	16.8205	9.1189	0.7315

Table IV. Speed-up Ratios for The Lamb Wave Problem

Mesh/	Speed-up Ratio		
Dimension	Scalar Computations	Automatic Vectorization	Super-Vectorization
23x23x10x2 = 10.580	1	1.80	1.86
46x10x2 = 42.320	1	15.03	21.00

In this problem, the net speed-up for the total minimization problem was an impressive factor of 21 for the
fine mesh case (46x46). It was noted that the speed-up
due to super-vectorization was a factor of almost 65 in
the function and gradient evaluation routine for this
problem. As for the coarser mesh version (23x23) of the
Lamb wave problem, the improvement was relatively
smaller, i.e. a factor of 1.86 only. This clearly
reflects the fact that the CYBER 205 has a slower vector
start-up time and its performance efficiency strongly
dependent on the vector length.

In this study, it is demonstrated that a sizable
reduction in the CPU time can be achieved by automatic
and then manual vectorization of the nonlinear conjugate
gradient method when it is applied to solve large scale
meteorological problems. Further research should
concentrate on other applications of vectorization of
large scale optimization problems using the nonlinear
conjugate gradient method such as in computational
chemistry, structural optimization, network optimization, etc.

Having vectorized the nonlinear conjugate **gradient** method, the next logical step is to multi-task it. Further research work can be carried out to take advantage of the multiprocessing capabilities of some supercomputers and exploit the inherent parallelism of the nonlinear conjugate gradient method.

7. REFERENCES

1. Beale, E.M.L., A derivation of conjugate gradients in Lootsma, F.A., ed., Numerical Methods for Nonlinear Optimization, Academic press, London, 1977, pp.39-43.

2. Bertsekas, D.P., Constrained Optimization and Lagrange Multiplier Methods, Academic Press, 1982, pp. 395.

3. Fletcher, R. and Reeves, C.M., Function Minimization by conjugate gradients, Computer Journal 7, 1964, pp. 149-165.

4. Gill, P.E. and Murray, W., Conjugate-gradient methods for large scale optimization, Tech. Report SOL 79-15, Systems Optimization Lab., Dept of Operations Research, Standford, 1979, 40 pages.

5. Hestenes, M.R. and E. Stiefel, Methods of Conjugate-gradient for solving linear systems, Research Journal of the National Bureau of Standards, 49, 1952, pp. 409-436.

6. Lootsma, F.A., State-of-the-art in parallel unconstrained optimization in Parallel Computing 85, M. Feilmeir, E. Joubert, and V. Schendel (eds.), North Holland, 1986, pp. 157-163.

7. Navon, I.M., FEUDX: A two stage, high-accuracy, finite-element FORTRAN program for solving the shallow-water equations, computers and Geosciences, 13, No. 3, 1987, pp. 255-285.

8. Navon, I.M. and R. de Villiers, GUSTAF - A Quasi-Newton nonlinear ADI FORTRAN IV Program for solving the shallow-water equations with augmented-Lagrangians, Computers and Geosciences, 12, 2, 1986, pp. 151-173.

9. Navon, I.M. and D.M. Legler, Conjugate-gradient methods for large-scale minimization in meteorology, Monthly Weather Review, 115, 1987, pp. 1479-1502.

72

10. Navon, I.M., P.K.H. Phua, and M. Ramamurthy, Vectorization of conjugate-gradient methods for Large-scale Minimization, Tech. Report FSU-SCRI-87-43, Supercomputer Computations Research Institute, Florida State University, August 1987, 30 pages.

11. Perry, A., A modified conjugate gradient algorithm, Discussion Paper 229, Center for Mathematical Studies in Economics and Management Science, Northwestern University, Evanston, Illinois, 1976.

12. Polak, E. and G. Ribiere, Note sur la convergence de methods de directions conjugres, Revue Francaise Informat, Recherche Operationelle 16, 1969, pp. 35-43.

13. Powell, M.J.D., Restart procedure for the con-jugate-gradient method, Math. Programming, 12, 1977, pp. 241-254.

14. Schnabel, R.B., Parallel computing in optimization, Computational Mathematical Programming 15, Nato ASI Series, F.K. Schittkowsky (ed.), Spring-Verlag, 1985, pp.357 -381.

15. Shanno, D.F., Conjugate gradient methods with inexact searches, Math. of Operations Research, 3, 1976, pp. 244-256.

16. Shanno, D.F. and K.H. Phua, Matrix conditioning and nonlinear optimization, Math. Programming, 14, 1978, pp. 149-160.

17. Shanno, D.F. and K.H. Phua, Remark on algorithm 500, ACM Trans. on Math. Software, 6,4, 1980, pp. 618-622.

SUPERCOMPUTER ORIENTED NUMERICAL ALGORITHMS FOR SPARSE MATRIX COMPUTATION

Takashi NODERA

Department of Mathematics
Faculty of Science and Technology
Keio University
3-14-1 Hiyoshi Kohoku, Yokohama 223
JAPAN

ABSTRACT

In recent years, numerical linear algebra plays a significant part of large scale scientific computing since powerful supercomputers become available. In this paper, we shall discuss the recent development of numerical algorithms for sparse matrix computation. Algorithms considered here include a new Preconditioned Conjugate Gradient (PCG) like procedure for solving sparse nonsymmetric systems of linear equations. Most of the algorithm is trivially vectorizable with a vector length equal to the full dimension of systems of linear equations. Consequently, magnificent savings of computational work are expected for supercomputers with vector processors. At last, we report on some numerical experiments for some of the important standard boundary value problems of the partial differential equation.

1. INTRODUCTION

Almost ten years ago, the first CRAY-1 supercomputer was set up to Los Alamos National Laboratory, and after that, supercomputers with vector processors have become worldwide and important roll in many area of the numerical solution of large scale computing. In recent years, the approach of high performance of Japanese supercomputers such as Hitachi (S810 and S820), NEC (SX-1 and SX-2) and Fujitsu (FACOM VP200 and VP400) is having an effective consequence on this area. Although we have a large potential gain accomplished for a lot of numerical problem by using supercomputers with vector processors as compared with using scalar computers, this potential gain can often be gotten by cautious choice of algorithms. This is especially true for the iterative algorithms

for solving the large and sparse linear systems of equations.

In this paper, we consider the solution of linear systems of algebraic equations:

$$Ax = b \tag{1.1}$$

where A is a large and sparse nonsingular matrix. This system frequently arises in the world of scientific and engineering applications, as in the solution of partial differential equations using finite difference and finite element approximations.

In general, we have two classes of numerical procedures for solving the above linear systems of equations, such as direct and iterative method. In recent years, both procedures have been extensive development which have produced significant improvements in computational efficiency. Historically speaking, iterative procedures have been very powerful solvers, if the coefficient matrix A is large and sparse. For instance, we consider the three dimension problems whose matrices is very large order and sparse elements structure. For these problems, the direct solvers such as Gaussian elimination and LU decomposition suffer from fill-in to such a matter that they can not be solved on the fine mesh to a reasonable cost even on the presently available the most effective supercomputers. On the other hand, the iterative solvers for solving the large sparse systems are better suited than the direct solvers, since they do not suffer from fill-in and they only require much less storage and reasonable computational cost at each iteration. In this paper, we survey some of our work on the recent development of iterative solvers which are designed to be effective when used on the supercomputers with vector processors.

A brief summery of the contents of this paper is as follows: In section 2, we describe iterative procedure, known as Preconditioned Conjugate Gradient (PCG) algorithm[1,4,14,28]. If A is symmetric and positive definite matrix, the PCG algorithm is a very popular and powerful solver. When A is symmetric and indefinite matrix, the conjugate residual algorithm[5] may be useful solver. If A is nonsymmetric and nonsingular matrix, the PCG algorithm for normal equations may converge slowly, in which case we need an effective preconditoner for the original coefficient matrix[11,18]. In section 3, we describe an overview of recent development in the conjugate gradient like algorithms, such as Bi-Conjugate Gradient (BCG) algorithm[7] and Conjugate Gradient Squared (CGS) algorithm[27], for solving nonsymmetric linear systems of equations. Especially, the conjugate gradient squared algorithm is pretty good solver which is efficient and easy to implement for the supercomputers with vector processors. In section 4, we consider the use of preconditioning in conjunction with the above techniques. We survey the recent results about approximate LU factorizations for nonsymmetric matrix. Finally, we also present the numerical experiments for solving the nonsymmetric linear systems of equations arising from the convective diffusion problem.

2. PRECONDITIONED CONJUGATE GRADIENT ALGORITHM

The conjugate gradient algorithm was developed in 1952 by Hestenes and Stiefel[9]. Magnificent discussions of this algorithm have appeared by several authors[1,4,11,12,14,18,22,28]. The conjugate gradient algorithm is a direct method if we use exact calculation. However, in practice, when we use finite precision, it behaves like an iterative procedure. Nowadays, the conjugate gradient algorithm is regarded as an iterative procedure for a system of linear equations. The theory of the conjugate gradient algorithm is well known and is presented in the lots of papers[1,4,9,14,15,22].

The efficiency of the classical conjugate gradient algorithm may be improved by using of some accelerated form such as preconditioned.

We consider the numerical solution of the equation $Ax = b$, where A is a $n \times n$ symmetric and positive definite matrix. We transform the original system of equations (1.1) into the following equivalent form:

$$BAx = Bb, \qquad (2.1)$$

where the matrix B is often called a preconditioning matrix or preconditioner. We should require the matrix B to approach the inverse of original matrix A which satisfies $\text{cond}(BA) \leq \text{cond}(A)$, where $\text{cond}(\cdot)$ is a spectral condition number.

Applying the classical conjugate gradient algorithm[9,14,28] to the above equivalent equation, we can obtain the following preconditioned conjugate gradient algorithm[1,11,12,13,14,28].

[PCG ALGORITHM]

Let x_0 be any initial approximation to the exact solution $\tilde{x}$, compute initial residual: $r_0 = b - Ax_0$ and put $p_0 = b_0 B r_0$, where B is any symmetric positive definite matrix. Then for $k = 0, 1, 2, 3, \ldots$, compute

$$x_{k+1} = x_k + \alpha_k p_k \qquad (2.2a)$$

$$r_{k+1} = r_k - \alpha_k A p_k \qquad (2.2b)$$

$$p_{k+1} = p_k + \beta_k B r_{k+1} \qquad (2.2c)$$

$$\alpha_k = 1/(p_k, A p_k) \qquad (2.2d)$$

$$\beta_k = 1/(r_{k+1}, B r_{k+1}). \qquad (2.2e)$$

We note that in this algorithm, an upper bound of the iteration counts can be given as follows[1,4,14].

$$k = \frac{1}{2} \sqrt{\text{cond}(BA)} \log_e(2/\epsilon), \qquad (2.3)$$

where ϵ is a error tolerance criterion. This upper bound frequently is excessively

pessimistic.

The convergence of this algorithm depends on the eigenvalues' distribution for the preconditoned system. If the eigenvalues of the coefficient matrix are clustered in a small number of groups, the preconditioned conjugate gradient will converge sufficiently fast, in a small number of iterations equal to the number of clustered groups. In order to speed up the convergence of this algorithm, we must require that the matrix B is chosen a good sparse approximation as inverse of the original matrix A in some sense, minimizing the spectral condition number cond(BA). Moreover, we also need that the matrix-vector product Bv is easily calculated. Namely, the matrix B has to be determined between preserving sparsity and getting the best approximate inverse of A. The influence of the preconditioning will be further discussed in the section 5.

Theoretically, the preconditioned conjugate gradient algorithm also terminates in n iterations, but it is not so important for large and sparse systems of equations. Because in practice, the preconditioned conjugate gradient algorithm converges in considerably fewer steps than n iterations, if you can obtain a good preconditioner B[1,4,8,11,12,13,28].

3. CONJUGATE GRADIENT LIKE ALGORITHM

The preconditioned conjugate gradient algorithm is not applicable to nonsymmetric indefinite matrices, because the minimization property of the conjugate gradient procedure is not valid for nonsymmetric indefinite matrices. The last over thirty years, it has been enlarged to nonsymmetric matrices by applying the conjugate gradient algorithm to normal equations:

$$A^T A x = A^T b$$

or

$$\begin{cases} AA^T u = b, \\ x = A^T u. \end{cases}$$

In 1978, Kershow[11] recommended the use of conjugate gradient procedure to solve the normal equations formed after preconditioning the original nonsymmetric system of equations. Nodera and Takahasi[18] also proposed several variants of the preconditioned conjugate gradient algorithm for nonsymmetric systems of equations. However, the disadvantage of this approach is that the condition number of the normal equation is the almost square of that of the original system of equations, and then we require more work of computation. Moreover, the spectrum of normal equations is usually spread out.

The generalization of the conjugate gradient algorithm to nonsymmetric and indefinite systems of equations which avoided the use of the normal equations was proposed by many researchers. The first one which is called the generalized conjugate gradient algorithm was presented by Concus and Golub[3] and Widlund[30].

SUMMARY OF CONJUGATE GRADIENT LIKE ALGORITHM		
Algorithm	Convergence Domain	Work and Storage
Conjugate Gradient for Normal Equations	General	Fixed, $A^T A$
Generalized Conjugate Residual (GCR)	M: positive definite	Increase
ORTHOMIN(q), $q \geq 0$	M: positive definite	Fixed
GCR(q), $q \geq 0$	M: positive definite	Fixed
AXEL-GCR (AXEL-LS)	M: positive definite	Increase
AXEL-GCR(q), $q \geq 0$	M: positive definite	Fixed
ORTHODIR	General	Increase
ORTHODIR(q), $q \geq 2$	$M = I$	Fixed
Bi-Conjugate Gradient (BCG)	General	Fixed
Conjugate Gradient Squared (CGS)	General	Fixed
AXEL-Galerkin	M: positive definite	Increase
Generalized Conjugate Gradient (GCG)	$M = I$	Fixed
ORTHORES	M: positive definite	Increase
ORTHORES(q), $q \geq 2$	$M = I$	Fixed
Full Orthogonalization Method (FOM)	M: positive definite	Increase
Incomplete Orthogonalization Method(q)	$M = I$	Fixed
DFOM	M: positive definite	Increase
DIOM(q), $q \geq 2$	$M = I$	Fixed
Generalized Minimal Residual (GMRES)	M: positive definite	Increase
GMRES(q), $q \geq 0$	M: positive definite	Fixed

Table 3.1 Summary of Conjugate Gradient Like Algorithms and Their Properties. $A = M - R$, where $M = (A + A^T)/2$ and $R = -(A - A^T)/2$.

Axelsson[2], Eisenstat et al.[5], Saad[23], Saad et al.[24], Saunders et al.[25] and Young and Jea[31,32] proposed a number of conjugate gradient like algorithm for more general problems. Each of these algorithms has an appropriate minimization property, but requires the storage of all previous search vectors. In some of these procedures, there exists truncated or restart versions. However, we still have the possibility of breakdown of these procedures.

In Table 3.1, We summarize the list of conjugate gradient like algorithms and their properties.

3.1 Bi-Conjugate Gradient Algorithm

One another generalization of the conjugate gradient algorithm is the bi-conjugate gradient algorithm. The bi-conjugate gradient algorithm was originally proposed by Fletcher[7] and has been investigated by several researchers[10,13,19,23]. In this section, we introduce how the bi-conjugate gradient algorithm can be derived from the classical conjugate gradient algorithm.

We already know that the conjugate gradient algorithm can not be applicable to nonsymmetric systems. Instead of solving the equation (1.1), we now consider to solve the following equivalent system with $2n \times 2n$ coefficient matrix:

$$\widetilde{A}u = \widetilde{b}, \tag{3.1}$$

where

$$\widetilde{A} = \begin{pmatrix} A & 0 \\ 0 & A^T \end{pmatrix}, \qquad u = \begin{pmatrix} x \\ \widetilde{x} \end{pmatrix}, \qquad \widetilde{b} = \begin{pmatrix} b \\ b \end{pmatrix}.$$

In order to reduce the equation (3.1) to symmetric system, we need to consider the symmetrizar of the matrix $\widetilde{A}$ which as follows:

$$\widetilde{S} = \begin{pmatrix} 0 & I \\ I & 0 \end{pmatrix}.$$

Applying the classical conjugate gradient algorithm[9] to the equation (3.1) by using the inner product with the above symmetrizar:

$$(\cdot, \cdot)_{\widetilde{S}} \equiv (\widetilde{S}\cdot, \cdot) \equiv (\cdot, \widetilde{S}\cdot), \tag{3.2}$$

we can obtain the bi-conjugate gradient algorithm as follows.

[BCG ALGORITHM]

Let x_0 be any initial approximation to the exact solution $\widetilde{x}$, compute initial residual: $r_0 = b - Ax_0$ and put $\widehat{p}_0 = \widehat{r}_0 = p_0 = r_0$. Then for $k = 0, 1, 2, 3, \ldots$, compute

$$x_{k+1} = x_k + \alpha_k p_k \tag{3.3a}$$

$$r_{k+1} = r_k - \alpha_k A p_k \tag{3.3b}$$

$$\widehat{r}_{k+1} = \widehat{r}_k - \alpha_k A^T \widehat{p}_k \tag{3.3c}$$

$$p_{k+1} = r_{k+1} + \beta_k p_k \tag{3.3d}$$

$$\widehat{p}_{k+1} = \widehat{r}_{k+1} + \beta_k \widehat{p}_k \tag{3.3d}$$

$$\alpha_k = (r_k, \widehat{r}_k)/(Ap_k, \widehat{p}_k) \tag{3.3e}$$

$$\beta_k = (r_{k+1}, \widehat{r}_{k+1})/(r_k, \widehat{r}_k). \tag{3.3f}$$

Since the inner product (3.2) is symmetric and linear form, but not positive definite, the bi-conjugate gradient algorithm is not the conjugate gradient algorithm, only an oblique projection procedure. The bi-conjugate gradient algorithm accordingly does not have a minimization properties as does the original conjugate gradient algorithm. In general, the bi-conjugate gradient algorithm converges faster than the conjugate gradient algorithm applied to normal equations, since it works on the original linear system of equations. However, it may have the possibility of breakdown with $\alpha_k = 0$ (or $\beta_k = 0$) and the existence of numerical instability before the approximate solution is found. If the BCG algorithm does not beak down within k ($\leq n$) iterations, then we have the convergence of this algorithm and we are able to obtain good numerical results. In practice, the bi-conjugate gradient algorithm is actually powerful solver for nonsymmetric and indefinite linear systems of equations, when it is combined with good preconditionings. In the next section, we will present another useful variant of the bi-conjugate gradient algorithm.

3.2 Conjugate Gradient Squared Algorithm

As an alternative to the bi-conjugate gradient algorithm, we can give the conjugate gradient squared (CGS) algorithm which was also developed to deal with the nonsymmetric and indefinite linear systems of equations. The conjugate gradient squared algorithm was firstly developed by Sonneveld[27]. The performance of the conjugate gradient squared algorithm and its numerical experiments have been given by Nodera[16,17].

The conjugate gradient squared algorithm is generated through the bi-conjugate gradient procedure, and the basic recurrence formulas is described as follows.

[CGS ALGORITHM]

Let $\overline{x}_0$ be any initial approximation to the exact solution $\widetilde{x}$, compute initial residual: $\overline{r}_0 = b - A\overline{x}_0$ and put $\overline{p}_0 = r_0 = e_0 = \overline{r}_0$. Then for $k = 0, 1, 2, 3, \ldots$, compute

$$\overline{x}_{k+1} = \overline{x}_k + \alpha_k(e_k + h_{k+1}) \tag{3.4a}$$

$$h_{k+1} = e_k - \alpha_k A\overline{p}_k \tag{3.4b}$$

$$\overline{r}_{k+1} = \overline{r}_k - \alpha_k A(e_k + h_{k+1}) \tag{3.4c}$$

$$e_{k+1} = \overline{r}_{k+1} + \beta_k h_{k+1} \tag{3.4d}$$

$$\overline{p}_{k+1} = e_{k+1} + \beta_k(h_{k+1} + \beta_k \overline{p}_k) \tag{3.4e}$$

$$\alpha_k = (r_0, \overline{r}_k)/(r_0, A\overline{p}_k) \tag{3.4f}$$

$$\beta_k = (r_0, \overline{r}_{k+1})/(r_0, \overline{r}_k). \tag{3.4g}$$

We remark that the conjugate gradient squared algorithm is mathematical equivalent to the bi-conjugate gradient algorithm. It is of interest to describe that the conjugate gradient squared algorithm has a superior feature rather than the BCG algorithm for the rate of convergence. Actually, the conjugate gradient squared algorithm has a great reduction of the number of iteration to converge, while its computational work and storage slightly increase per iteration. In particular, the convergence of conjugate gradient squared algorithm is almost twice as fast as that of bi-conjugate gradient algorithm. Consequently, we save the much computational expense on the supercomputers.

In **Table** 3.2, we summarize the detailed work and storage costs per iteration for the several conjugate gradient like algorithms (including BCG and CGS algorithm).

Essentially, BCG as the conjugate gradient algorithm is, we may have the possibility of breakdown and the numerical instability of the procedure. To overcome these difficulties and make the algorithm more effective, we need to have the better rate of convergence of the conjugate gradient squared algorithm using the efficient preconditioning.

ALGORITHM	WORK/ITERATION	STORAGE
GCR	$(3(k+1)+4)n, Av$	$(2(k+2)+2)n$
ORTHOMIN(q)	$(3q+4)n, Av$	$(2q+4)n$
GCR(q)	$((3/2)q+4)n, Av$	$(2q+4)n$
BCG	$7n, Av, A^T v$	$6n$
CGS	$8n, 2 \times Av$	$7n$

Table 3.2 Comparisons of Work per Iterations and Storage Requirement of Different CG Like Algorithm.

4. PRECONDITIONING

As noted in previous section 2, the preconditioning is the transformation of original system (1.1) to the equivalent preconditioned form (2.2). It is well known that the success of the conjugate gradient like algorithms depends on the quality of preconditionings. With proper preconditioning, the number of iterations to get an approximate solution is reduced to the range that the total time decreases. Accordingly, the rate of convergence depends on what kind of preconditioners should be used.

Recent work on the preconditioning has been regarded as the various choice of preconditioner B, which depends on the rate of convergence, storage requirement and computational time. There are two developments in the evolution of preconditioning. One effective class of preconditioning is a splitting[1,6,14,28] of the matrix and other is an approximate factorization[8,11,12,30] of the original matrix. Obtaining the preconditioner B through the splitting of matrix has been developed by Evans[6], Axelsson[1], Takahasi and Nodera[28] and Nodera[14]. The incomplete Cholesky factorization was introduced by Meijerink and van der Vorst[12], and examined by Kershow[11], and many other researchers. The modified incomplete Cholesky factorization was introduced by Gustafsson[8]. In lately, the possibility of different preconditioner from a computational point of view has been presented for vector or parallel computers, by van der Vorst[29] and Poole and Ortega[21].

For the nonsymmetric systems of linear equations, we can usually use the preconditioners which consist of an incomplete LU (ILU) factorization[12] and a modified incomplete LU (MILU) factorization[8]. The incomplete LU factorization of the coefficient matrix A can be given as follows.

$$A = LU + R, \qquad (4.1)$$

where R is the error matrix which devoted to dropping high level terms, and L and U are a lower triangular matrix, an upper triangular matrix, respectively. Since these matrices normally hold on the sparsity pattern of the original coefficient matrix, it is apparent that we need not caluculate all the elements of matrix. In many case, these preconditioners can be calculated quite easily by using Gaussian elimination.

There are conventionally three different determinations of the preconditioning that could be used as follows:

$$\begin{cases} L^{-1}AU^{-1}u = L^{-1}b, \\ \quad x = U^{-1}u \end{cases} \qquad (4.2)$$

$$(LU)^{-1}Ax = (LU)^{-1}b \qquad (4.3)$$

$$\begin{cases} A(LU)^{-1}u = b, \\ x = (LU)^{-1}u. \end{cases} \qquad (4.4)$$

Each form of the preconditioning leads to different preconditioned systems. We recommend the right preconditioning, because the residual of the preconditioned system is equivalent to the residual of the original system (1.1) as follows:

$$r_k = b - A(LU)^{-1}u_k = b - Ax_k. \qquad (4.5)$$

Useful vectorization techniqes of the preconditionings on the supercomputers are described by Van der Vorst[29], Simon[26] and Poole and Ortega[21].

Unfortunately, it is difficult to explain effect of the preconditionings for the nonsymmetric linear systems of equations, because the most of preconditioners are heuristically derived from the conceptions of approximation to the original matrix and from these techniques only known to be adequate for symmetric positive definite systems. We must to say that for the nonsymmetric systems, the technique of preconditioning is more part of an art than that of a science.

5. NUMERICAL EXPERIMENTS

In this section, we examine the performance of the conjugate gradient squared algorithm and other conjugate gradient like algorithms in solving a nonsymmetric

β	algorithm					
	BCG		CGS		ORTHOMIN(1)	
	Iters.	Mults.	Iters.	Mults.	Iters.	Mults.
10	61	2467023	40	1678560	119	3039855
100	29	1172847	17	713388	38	970710
1000	24	970632	12	503568	24	613080

Table 5.1 Number of Iterations and Number of Multiplications for Convergence ($\epsilon = 10^{-14}$) When Applied to ILU Preconditioning ($h = 1/40$).

linear system of equations arising from the discretization of the partial differential equation. All the numerical tests were done in double precision arithmetic (55 bit mantissa).

β	algorithm					
	BCG		CGS		ORTHOMIN(1)	
	Iters.	Mults.	Iters.	Mults.	Iters.	Mults.
10	37	1496391	22	923208	51	1302795
100	30	1213290	16	671424	35	894075
1000	24	970632	12	503568	24	613080

Table 5.2 Number of Iterations and Number of Multiplications for Convergence ($\epsilon = 10^{-14}$) When Applied to $MILU$ Preconditioning ($h = 1/40$).

We consider the boundary value problem:

$$\Delta u + \beta u_x = f \qquad \text{in } \Omega$$
$$u = xy(1-x)(1-y) \qquad \text{on } \partial\Omega \tag{5.1}$$

where Ω is unite square: $[0,1] \times [0,1]$ with Dirichlet boundary conditions and β is a constant. In our trials, we took $f = 2x(x-1) + y(y-1)\{2 - \beta(1-2x)\}$ and a 39 × 39 uniform mesh of discretization points on Ω ($h = 1/40$). We discretized the grid points using standard 5-point central difference approximation. We examined three cases of numerical experiments with $\epsilon \, (= \|r_k\|/\|r_0\|) \leq 10^{-14}$, corresponding to $\beta = 10, 100, 1000$.

In order to give an overview over the general performance of conjugate gradient like algorithms with the incomplete factorization preconditioning, we studied to use the natural ordering and a level 0 incomplete LU or $MILU$ factorization.

ITERATIONS

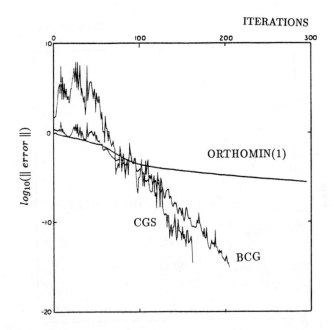

Figure 5.1 The Behavior of Residual vs. The Number of Iterations, $h = 1/40, \beta = 10$, Nonpreconditioning.

To compare the efficiency of each of the conjugate gradient like algorithms, it is necessary to consider the computational work per iterations as well as the number of iterations required to convergence. One way of estimating this computational work is to count the number of arithmetic operations, especially multiplications, during the iterations.

In Table 5.1 and 5.2, we compare the total number of iterations and the total number of multiplications required to decrease the error tolerance, when applied the conjugate gradient like algorithms with the incomplete factorization preconditioning to this problem. However, all the overhead for computing the incomplete LU factorization and the modified incomplete LU factorization is excluded in these operation counts.

In Figure 5.1 and 5.2, we also show the behavior of the residual norm versus the number of iterations for the different conjugate gradient like algorithms.

These results show that the ORTHOMIN(1) without preconditioning converges very poorly. The conjugate gradient squared method with the modified incomplete LU factorization converges considerably better than the other conjugate gradient like procedures. For the conjugate gradient squared algorithm, more comprehensive numerical experiments are given in Nodera[16,17].

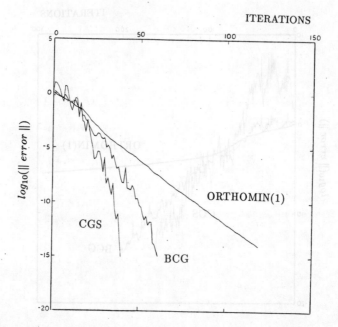

Figure 5.2 The Behavior of Residual vs. The Number of Iterations, $h = 1/40, \beta = 10,$ *ILU* Preconditioning.

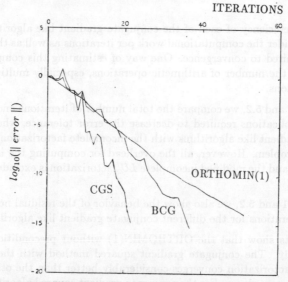

Figure 5.3 The Behavior of Residual vs. The Number of Iterations, $h = 1/40, \beta = 10,$ *MILU* Preconditioning.

6. CONCLUSION

we have described the development of the conjugate gradient like algorithms which are currently being used to solve problems resulting from the discretization of the boundary value problem of the partial differential equations. These algorithms which mentioned here are efficient solvers when used on the supercomputers with vector processors. In particular, the conjugate gradient squared algorithm is designed to be very effective for solving nonsymmetric and indefinite linear systems of algebraic equations. Mathematically speaking, the conjugate gradient squared algorithm is just a reconstruction of the classical process of the bi-conjugate gradient algorithm. However, it has computationally superior properties. Based on the numerical experiments given here, we belive that the conjugate gradient squared algorithm with the $MILU$ factorization is the most effective solver for this type of problems. Namely, the greatly improved of the rate of convergence is obtained by the conjugate gradient squared algorithm with a proper preconditioning means that the numerical solution of nonsymmetric and indefinite linear systems of algebraic equations is more realizable now than ever before.

REFERENCES

1. Axelsson, O., *Solution of Linear Systems of Equations*, in "Lecture Notes in Math., 572," Springer-Verlag, 1977, pp. 1–51.

2. Axelsson, O., *Conjugate Gradient Type Methods for Unsymmetric and Inconsistent Systems of Linear Equations*, Linear Algebra and its Appl. 29 (1980), 1–16.

3. Concus, P. and Golub, G. H., *A Generalized Conjugate Gradient Method for Nonsymmetric Systems of Linear Equations*, in "Lecture Notes in Economics and Mathematical Systems, 134," Springer-Verlag, 1976, pp. 56–65.

4. Concus, P. , Golub, G. H. and O'Leary, D. R., *A Generalized Conjugate Gradient Method for Numerical Solution of Elliptic Partial Differential Equations*, in "Sparse Matrix Computation (Banch, J. R. and Rose, D. J. eds.)," Academic Press, 1976, pp. 309–332.

5. Eisenstat, S. C., Elman, H. C. and Schultz, M. H., *Variational Iterative Methods for Nonsymmetric Systems of Linear Equations*, SIAM J. Numer. Anal. 20 (1983), 345–357.

6. Evans, D. J., *The Use of Preconditioning in Iterative Methods for Solving Linear Equation with Symmetric Positive Definite Matrices*, J. IMA 4 (1968), 295–314.

7. Flecher, R., *Conjugate Gradient Methods for Indefinite Systems*, in "Lecture Notes in Math.," 1976, pp. 73–89.

8. Gustafsson, I., *A Class of First Order Factorizations*, BIT 18 (1978), 142–156.

9. Hestenes, M. R. and Stiefel, E., *Methods of Conjugate Gradients for Solving Linear Systems*, J. Research Nat. Bur. Standards 49 (1952), 409–435.

10. Jacobs, D. A. H., *The Exploitation of Sparsity of Iterative Methods*, in "Sparse Matrices and their Uses(Duff, I. F. ed.)," Academic Press, 1981, pp. 191–222.

11. Kershow, D. S., *The Incomplete Cholesky-Conjugate Gradient Method for the Iterative Solution of Systems of Linear Equations*, J. of Comp. Physics 26 (1978), 43–65.

12. **Meijerink**, J. A. and Van der Vorst, H. A., *An Iterative Solution Method for Linear Systems of Which the Coefficient Matrix is Symmetric M-matrix*, Math. Comp. **31** (1977), 148–162.

13. Natori, M. and Nodera, T., *Iterative Methods for Large Scale Matrix Problems*, in Japanese, Transaction of Information Processing **28** (1987), 1452–1459.

14. Nodera, T., *PCG Methods for a Large Sparse Matrix*, in "Seminar on Mathematical Science, **7**," in Japanese, Keio University, 1983.

15. _____, *Data Flow Analysis of Orthogonal Properties on the Conjugate Gradient and the Lanczos Algorithm*, in "Numerical Mathematics and Applications (Vichnevetsky, R. and Vignes, J. eds.)," North-Holland, 1986, pp. 95-103.

16. _____, *New Variant of BCG Method for Solving Nonsymmetric Systems*, in "Advances in Computer Methods for Partial Differential Equations VI (Stepleman, R. S. and Vichnevetsky, R. eds.)," IMACS, 1987, pp. 130–135.

17. _____, *The Use of a CGS Method for the Convective Diffusion Problem*, in "Computational Techniques and Applications (Noye, J. and Fletcher, C. eds.)," North-Holland, 1988, pp. 529–538.

18. Nodera, T. and Takahasi, H., *Preconditioned Conjugate Gradient Algorithms for Nonsymmetric Matrix*, in "Scientific Computing (Stepleman, R. S. ed.)," North-Holland, 1983, pp. 173-180.

19. O'Leary, D. P., *The Block Conjugate Gradient Algorithm and Related Methods*, Linear Algebra and its Appl. **29** (1980), 293–322.

20. Pages, C. C. and Saunders, M. A., *Solution of Sparse Indefinite Systems of Linear Equations*, SIAM J. Numer. Anal. **12** (1975), 617–629.

21. Poole, E. L. and Ortega, J. M., *Multicolor ICCG Methods for Vector Computer*, SIAM J. Numer. Anal. **24** (1987), 1394–1418.

22. Reid, J. K., *On the Method of Conjugate Gradients for the Solution of Large Sparse Systems of Linear Equations*, in "Large Sparse Sets of Linear Equations (Reid J. K. ed.)," Academic Press, 1971, pp. 231-254.

23. Saad, Y., *The Lanczos Biorthogonalization Algorithm and Oblique Projection Methods for Solving Large Unsymmetric Systems*, SIAM J. Numer. Anal. **19** (1982), 458–506.

24. Saad, Y. and Schultz, M. H., *GMRES, A Generalized Minimal Residual Algorithm for Solving Nonsymmetric Linear Systems*, SIAM J. Sci. Stat. Comput. **7** (1986), 856–869.

25. Saunders, M. A., Simon, H. D. and Yip, E. L., *Two Conjugate Gradient Type Methods for Sparse Unsymmetric Linear Solutions*, Technical Report ETA-TR-1, 1984, Boeing Computer Service.

26. Simon, H. D., *Supercomputer Vectorization and Optimization Guide*, Report ETA-TR-22, 1984, Boeing Computer Services.

27. Sonneveld, P. S., *CGS, A Fast Lanczos Type Solver for Nonsymmetric Linear Systems*, Report 84–16, 1984, Delft University.

28. Takahasi, H. and Nodera, T., *New Variants of Conjugate Gradient Algorithm*, in "Numerical Methods for Engineering Vol. 1 (Absi, E., Glowinski, R. et al. eds.)," Dunod, 1980, pp. 209–219.

29. Van der Vorst, H. A., *A Vectorizable Variant of Some ICCG Methods*, SIAM J. Sci. Stat. Comput. **3** (1982), 350–356.

30. Widlund, O., *A Lanczos Method for a Class of Nonsymmetric Systems of Linear Equations*, SIAM J. Numer. Anal. **15** (1978), 801–812.

31. Young, D. M. and Jea, K. C., *Generalized Conjugate Gradient Acceleration of Nonsymmetrizable Iterative Methods*, Linear Algebra and its Appl. **34** (1980), 159–194.

32. Young, D, M., Jea, K. C. and Kincaid, D. R., *Accelerating Nonsymmetrizable Iterative Methods*, in "Elliptic Solvers II," Academic Press, 1984, pp. 323–342.

Calculation of pi to the 33 Million
Decimal Places as Benchmark and Heat Run Tests

Yasumasa Kanada

Computer Centre, University of Tokyo
Bunkyo-ku Yayoi 2-11-16, Tokyo 113, Japan

KEY WORDS : Calculation of pi, Benchmarking, FFT, arithmetic-geometric mean, Gauss-Legendre relation, statistical tests, Supercomputer

ABSTRACT

Program for calculating pi up to 33,554,414 decimal places were used for benchmarking and heat-run testing S-820 model 80 supercomputer. The program for pi calculation written in FORTRAN based on the new algorithm for pi, 4-th order convergent algorithm, which was discovered by Borwein in middle of 1980's. The computation took CPU times of 2 hours 47 minutes 49 seconds and 8 hours 34 seconds on the HITAC S-820 model 80 supercomputer (Dec. 1987) and HITAC S-810 model 20 (Aug. 1985) respectively. According to these figures, all over speed up factor of 2.86 was realized by the new supercomputer S-820 model 80 and the new optimizing FORTRAN E2 compiler. Here all over speed up factor means factor realized both hardware and software.

For generating pi up to 33 million decimal places, main memory of 256 Mb and 3/4Gb of Extended Storage for shorten I/O time were required. In order to benchmark the system performance, e.g. performances for the hardware and software including OS facilities, FORTRAN program which consumes nearly all the resources of main memory, Extended Storage and CPU time is favorable. In that sense, calculation of pi to many places is one of the best.

PERFORMANCE OF SUPERCOMPUTER VERSIONS OF NUMPAC

Ichizo Ninomiya
Chubu University, Kasugai, Aichi, 487 Japan

Yasuyo Hatano
Chukyo University, Yagoto, Nagoya, 466 Japan

ABSTRACT

The mathematical library NUMPAC (Nagoya University Mathematical
Package) has been constructed since 1971 by cooperation of members of
the Nagoya University Numerical Analysis Group. It is an all-round and
general purpose numerical package consisting of 1000 high quality sub-
routines which cover a vast field of linear algebra, nonlinear equation,
interpolation, Fourier analysis, numerical quadrature, ordinary differential equation, special function and nonnumerical processing. It has
been installed in 40 principal computing institutes of Japan and has
been utilized extensively.

From 1984 on, supercomputer versions of NUMPAC have been written
and, at present, there exist three versions each consisting of 50 sub-
rotines for linear algebra tuned respectively for machines of FUJITSU,
HITACHI and NEC. Recently, an overall speed test for these versions was
conducted. It turned out that the results obtained indicated high performance of NUMPAC decidedly. For example, a system of linear equations
with 1000 unknowns can be solved by LEQLUW in 0.6 to 1.4 seconds and
a computation for all the eigenpairs of a symmetric matrix can be carried
out in about 10 seconds.

REFERENCES

1. Ninomiya, I. and Hatano, Y.,"Mathematical Library NUMPAC"
   Jyohoshori, Vol.26,No.9,pp.1033-1042(1985)(in Japanese)

2. Ninomiya,I.,"Supercomputer and Mathematical Library
   Jyohoshori,Vol.27,No.11,pp.1235-1241(1986)(in Japanese)

3. Nagoya University Computation Center,"Manuals for Library
   Programs, NUMPAC versions, Vol.1,Vol.2"(1988)(in Japanese)

Part 3
Software Techniques for Supercomputing

VFP: Vectorized Interpreter of the Functional Programming Language FP

Compiling Optimizations through Program Transformations

Part 3
Software Techniques for Supercomputing

VFP: Vectorized Interpreter of the Functional Programming Language FP

Compiling Optimizations through Program Transformations

VFP:VECTORIZED INTERPRETER OF THE FUNCTIONAL PROGRAMMING LANGUAGE FP

Masaaki Shimasaki, Kenji Hirai and Takao Tsuda

Kyoto University

Kyoto, Japan

ABSTRACT

We have designed and implemented the VFP system, a vectorized interpreter of the functional programming language FP for a vector supercomputer FACOM VP-200. In our VFP system, data structures suitable for vector proccesing are adopted, and parallel type primitive functions such as 'distl', 'distr' or parallel type functional forms such as 'apply-to-all' are efficiently interpreted using vectorizing FORTRAN DO loops. We give methods to improve vectorization ratio using the FP algebra. Some results on performance evaluation of our VFP system are given.

1. INTRODUCTION

Although in the FP system there are many possibilities of high speed computation by parallel processing, a conventional implementation on a scalar computer cannot make use of this inherent parallelism. In the FP system on a conventional scalar computer, it is impossible to avoid word-at-a-time processing at run-time. In recent years, pipeline vector supercomputers become rather easily accessible and the motivation behind the present paper is to investigate the feasibility of pipeline vector processing approach in implementation of FP-like functional languages. We designed and implemented the VFP system (Vectorized FP Translater-Interpreter) for a vector supercomputer FACOM VP-200. In our VFP system, data structures suitable for vector processing are adopted, and parallel type primitive functions such as 'distl','distr' or parallel type functional forms such as 'apply-to-all' are efficiently interpreted using vectorizing FORTRAN DO loops. In section 2, we discuss about the significance of vector processing in the FP system, and basic strategy to attain high performance in the FP system using vector processing facility. In section 3, an overview of our VFP system is given. In section 4, we give some results on performance evaluation of our VFP system using 1) primitive functions, 2) basic functional forms and 3) program level functions.

Although current commercially available vector supercomputers are mainly designed for numerical computation (floating-point computations) rather than for non-numeric computation (other than floating-point computation), the VFP system attained a certain level of high performance.

2.THE FP SYSTEM AND VECTOR PROCESSING

2.1 Significance of Vector Processing in the FP System and Basic Idea behind the VFP System

The basic idea of Backus FP system[1] is to avoid word-at-a-time processing and the sequence data type plays an important role in the FP system. In the FP system there are sequence-transformation functions which can be executed in parallel. If the FP system is, however, implemented on a convectional scalar computer[2], all the computation is carried out by sequential manner. In recent years, pipeline vector computers become easily accessible computers. It is significant to investigate how such vector processing capability can be made use of in implementation of FP-like functional languages. If we adopt an array data structure to represent objects of the sequence type and the interpreter is written in FORTRAN DO loop, then parallel-type sequence-transformation operations such as 'apply-to-all' can be executed on vector processing unit.

2.2 High Speed Processing of 'Sequence' by Vector Processing
2.2.1 Data Structure in the VFP System
In order to realize high speed processing on vector supercomputers,

it is crucial to adopt a data structure suitable for pipeline operations. A programming language available on FACOM VP-200 is FORTRAN 77/VP only (an assembly language is not available), and an array data structure is used to represent data objects in the FP. A data object in the FP is either an atom or a sequence, and an object has following internal form:

atom cell:

type	value	length

sequence cell:

seq		length	pointer1	...	pointerN

In the current version of the VFP system, a data type of an atomic object is either integer or boolean. An extension to treat other atomic data type is under investigation. A sequence cell consists of the length information and pointers linked to object cells of elements.

2.2.2 Basic Form of Operation

If we use data structure given in the previous section, vector processing of an FP object is exemplified using an example of 'reverse' function. The corresponding part of the interpreter can be written in the following segment of FORTRAN program:

```
            A(NEW)='seq'
            A(NEW+2)=A(NOW+2)
      *VOCL  LOOP,NOVREC(A)
```

```
        DO   10   I=1,A(NOW+2)
        A(NEW+2+I )=A(NOW+3+A(NOW+2)-I )
     10  CONTINUE
```

NOW points to the data object to which the reverse function is applied and NEW points to the new object which is obtained as a result of the reverse operation. In the operation of reverse:<1, 2, 3>, the input and output of the 'reverse' function is illustrated in Fig. 1.

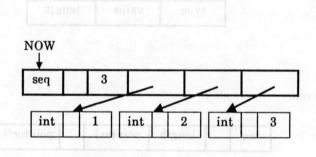

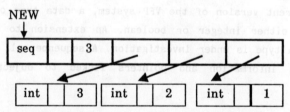

Fig. 1 Input and output of reverse function

In the above example, the *VOCL line indicates a compiler option which forces the compiler to vectorize the succeeding DO loop without paying attention to the data-dependency relation. Without this compiler option, the compiler cannot judge the data dependency relation which might prohibit vectorization.

2.3 Analysis of Vectorizable Part of Operations in the FP System

In the previous section we showed a data structure suitable for vector operation, and gave an example of vectorization in the 'sequence' operation. In this section we consider the vectorization of the functional form 'Apply-to-all'. Whether the operation can be vectorized or not depends on the type of primitive function which is the argument function of the 'apply-to-all'. If the argument function of the 'apply-to-all' functional form is one of arithmetic operations, e.g.

α + (apply '+' operation to all the elements of tuple),

then the length of elements in the sequence is the same and the operation is directly vectorizable. On the other hand, if the argument function is one of structure-transformation functions, their possible inhomogenuity in the FP objects (the length of elements may vary) makes simple vectorization difficult. For example, in the following example,

α reverse:⟨⟨2⟩,⟨1,2,3⟩,⟨3,4⟩⟩

=⟨reverse:⟨2⟩, reverse:⟨1,2,3⟩, reverse:⟨3,4⟩⟩

=⟨⟨2⟩,⟨3,2,1⟩,⟨4,3⟩⟩.

Thus the α reverse operation carried out applying the reverse operation in an elementwise fashion. In the case of α reverse, the functional form 'apply-to-all' itself cannot enjoy the effect of vectorization, but the element function 'reverse' can be carried out in vector operation mode.

Next lets us consider the case when the argument of 'apply-to-all' is 'concat'. As in the case of α reverse, elements of tuple of the nest level 1 may not have the same structure (inhomogeneous tuple) and only element-wise operation can be vectorized. In the VFP system, 'apply-to-all' can be vectorized when it is applied to one of the foollowing primitive functions:

selector function	(first, last, s)
test function	(atom, eq, null, length)
arithmetic function	(+, -, *, ÷)
logical function	(and, or, not)

```
            library routines          (mod, sine etc)
            miscellaneous functions   (id, iota)
```

As special cases the following operations

```
            /  +        (insert plus)
            /  or       (insert or)
            /  and      (insert and)
```

can also be vectorized.

2.4 A Method to Improve Vectorization Ratio in the FP System

It is well known as Amdahl's law that high vectorization ratio is crucial to attain high performance on vectorcomputers. In this section we show a method to improve the vectorization ratio when the argument function of the functional form 'apply-to-all' is one of the functional forms 'apply-to-all', 'construction' or 'condition'.

1) The case of nested 'apply-to-all's

First let us consider the case of nested ' apply-to-all', such as $\alpha(\alpha +)$:

Following the definition of the 'apply-to-all', the computation proceeds as follows:

$$\alpha (\alpha +):\langle\langle\langle1,2\rangle,\langle2,3\rangle,\langle\langle3,4\rangle\rangle\rangle$$
$$=\langle \alpha +:\langle\langle1,2\rangle,\langle2,3\rangle\rangle, \alpha +:\langle\langle3,4\rangle\rangle\rangle$$
$$=\langle\langle+:\langle1,2\rangle,+:\langle2,3\rangle\rangle,\langle+:3,4\rangle\rangle\rangle$$
$$=\langle\langle3,5\rangle,\langle7\rangle\rangle.$$

The operation cannot be vectorized as in the case when the structure-transforming function is applied to all the elements objects. When the VFP system encounters the nested 'apply-to-all' with function, e.g.+, then the system flattens the tuple and at the same time makes a record of length information of the original tuple as:

$$[concat, \alpha\ length]:\langle\langle\langle1, 2\rangle,\langle2, 3\rangle,\langle\langle3, 4\rangle\rangle\rangle$$
$$=\langle\langle\langle1, 2\rangle,\langle2, 3\rangle,\langle3, 4\rangle\rangle,\langle2, 1\rangle\rangle$$

If we apply $\alpha +$ to the first element, we have the following.

$$[\underline{\alpha + \circ 1}, 2] \underline{\circ} [concat, \underline{\alpha}\ length]:\langle\langle\langle1, 2\rangle,\langle2, 3\rangle,\langle\langle3, 4\rangle\rangle\rangle$$
$$=[\underline{\alpha + \circ 1}, 2]:\langle\langle\langle1, 2\rangle,\langle2, 3\rangle,\langle3, 4\rangle\rangle,\langle2, 1\rangle\rangle$$

$$=\langle \; \underline{\alpha \; +:\langle\langle 1, \; 2\rangle,\langle 2, \; 3\rangle,\langle 3, \; 4\rangle\rangle},\langle 2, \; 1\rangle\rangle$$
$$=\langle\underline{+:\langle 1, \; 2\rangle,+:\langle 2, \; 3\rangle,+:\langle 3, \; 4\rangle\rangle},\langle 2, \; 1\rangle\rangle$$
$$=\langle\langle 3, \; 5, \; 7\rangle,\langle 2, \; 1\rangle\rangle.$$

The underlined part of operation can be vectorized. The VFP system used the second element, the length information, and returns the correct result $\langle\langle 3, 5\rangle,\langle 7\rangle\rangle$. The same approach can be used to treat multiply nested 'apply-to-all' operations.

2) The use of FP alegebra

Now let us consider the combination of 'apply-to-all' and 'construction'. According to the original definition, we have

$$\alpha \; [f_1, \; f_2, \; \ldots, \; f_n]:\langle x_1, \; x_2, \; \ldots, \; x_n\rangle$$
$$=\langle[f_1, \; f_2, \; \ldots, f_n]: x_1, \; [f_1, \; f_2, \; \ldots, f_n]: x_2,$$
$$\ldots, \; [f_1, \; f_2, \; \ldots, f_n]: x_n\rangle$$
$$=\langle\langle f_1: x_1, \; \ldots, f_n:x_1\rangle, \; \ldots, \langle f_1:x_n, \; \ldots, f_n:x_n\rangle\rangle.$$

The operation cannot be vectorized. If we use the algebra of FP, we can transform the above equation into the vectorizable form:

$$\langle\langle f_1:x_1, \; \ldots, f_n:x_1\rangle, \; \ldots, \langle f_1:x_n, \; \ldots, f_n:x_n\rangle\rangle$$
$$=trans:\langle\langle f_1:x_1, \; \ldots, f_1:x_n\rangle, \; \ldots, \langle f_n:x_1, \; \ldots, f_n:x_n\rangle\rangle$$
$$=trans \circ \langle \; \alpha \; f_1:\langle x_1,x_2, \; \ldots, x_n\rangle, \; \ldots, $$
$$\alpha \; f_n:\langle x_1, \; x_2, \; \ldots, x_n\rangle\rangle$$
$$=trans \circ [\; \alpha \; f_1, \; \ldots, \; \alpha \; f_n]:\langle x_1, \; x_2, \; \ldots, x_n\rangle.$$

It should be noted that $\alpha \; f_i:\langle x_1, \; x_2, \; \ldots, x_n\rangle$ can be executed by vector operation and that the 'trans' operation itself is also vectorizable.

3) The use of gather/scatter operation

Let us consider the combination of 'apply-to-all' and 'condition'. Without loss of generality we can assume the following form:

$$\alpha \; (p \to q; \; r):\langle x_1, \; x_2, \; \ldots, x_n\rangle$$
$$=\langle(p \to q; \; r): x_1, \; (p \to q; \; r): x_2, \; \ldots, (p \to q; \; r): x_n\rangle.$$

Depending on the truth value of $p:x_i$, either $q:x_i$ or $r:x_i$ is evaluated. If we first compute the boolean vector

$$\alpha \; p:\langle x_1, x_2, \ldots, x_n \rangle,$$

then this vector can be used as a mask vector in gather/scatter operation and the total computation can be vectorized.

3. OVERVIEW OF THE VFP SYSTEM

3.1 VFP Translater

The VFP system consists of the VFP translator, the VFP interpreter and the garbage collector. In the VFP system we follow the syntax convention adopted by the Berkeley FP system in principle.

The grammar of the FP language is basically an LL(1) grammar and the current version of the VFP translater is implemented by the recursive descent technique using PL/I.

As an example we give the FP program for an inner product function and the corresponding intermediate codes.

FP program for inner product of vectors:

$$\{ip \equiv / + \circ \; \alpha \; * \circ \; trans\}$$

the intermediate codes for the portion of the inner product function

$trans
$apply
$*
$applyend
$rinsert
$+
$rinsertend

3.2 VFP Interpreter

3.2.1 The structure of the VFP Interpreter

The VFP interpreter has the storage for intermediate codes, the dynamic storage for object cells, five stacks and some registers as illustrated in Fig.2.

storage for
intermediate codes

dynamic storage for
objects

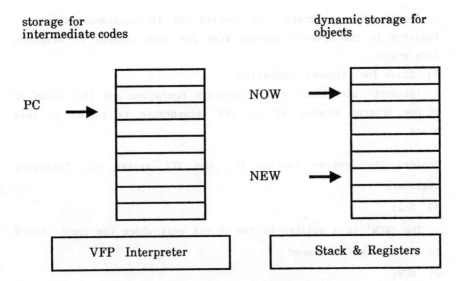

Fig.2 Schematic diagram of VFP interpreter

Five stacks in the VFP system are as follows:

1) Return Address Stack

When a user-defined function is invoked, the return address is pushed on this stack.

2) Stack for optimized execution of the nested 'apply-to-all' functional form

As we discussed in the section 2.4, the 'contact' operation is applied to flatten the tuple structure prior to 'apply-to-all' operation to attain high performance. The length information is saved on this stack so that the VFP system recover the correct tuple structure after the 'apply-to-all' operation.

3) Condition Stack

When the VFP system encounters a combination of 'apply-to-all' function form and 'conditional' form, the mask vector is stored on this stack.

4) Stack for 'Construction' functional form

'Construction' operation is carried out in an element-wise way. Position in the dynamic storage area for each element is saved on this stack.

5) Stack for 'Rinsert' Operation

'Rinsert' operation is a repetitive operation and the value of PC,the program counter of the VFP interpreter is stored on this stack.

Besides the program counter PC, the VFP system has following registers:

1) Now:

The 'NOW' is a pointer to the object cell where the input object to the function is stored.

2) NEW:

The 'NEW'is a pointer to the object cell where the output object of the function is to be created.

3) AF:

The AF register holds the nest level of the multiply nested 'apply-to-all' functional form.

3.2.2 Interpreting Process

The VFP interpreter repeats the following cycle:

1) to fetch an instruction of intermediate codes pointed by the program counter PC from the code storage, and

2) to apply necessary operations to the object in the object cell pointed by the 'NOW' pointer, and to create the result object at the position in the object cell pointed by the 'NEW' pointer,

3) to update the program counter PC and the object pointer 'NOW' and 'NEW'.

For primitive functions, operations done by the VFP system are the same with those defined by the original FP system, except for the 'apply-to-all' operation. When the operation is 'apply-to-all', the VFP system checks whether the involved operation can be efficiently executed by vector operation as discussed in 2.3 and 2.4. If the value of the AF register is positive, the effect of vector operation depends on the kind of involved operation and the VFP interpreter takes the most efficient action for each case. The execution process can be illustrated by the following example:

  process of execution of

a (a +):<<<1, 2>,<2, 3>>>,<<1, 3>>,<<<1, 0>>>

  1)execution of $apply,   AF=1
      length information:<3>
      object cell:<<<1, 2>,<2, 3>>,<<1, 3>>,<<1, 0>>>
  2) execution of $apply,   AF=2
      length information:<2, 1, 1>
      object cell:<<1, 2>,<2, 3>,<1, 3>,<1, 0>>
  3) execution of apply $+
      length information:<2, 1, 1>
      object cell:<3, 5, 4, 1>
  4) execution of $applyend, AF=1
      object cell:<<3, 5>, 4, 1>
  5) execution of $applyend, AF=0
      object cell:<<3, 5>, 4, 1> --> the final result.

3.3 Garbage Collector

In the implementation of the functional programming languages, it is important to provide a garbage collector for the dynamic storage area. The VFP system has a 'copy'-garbage collector for the object cell storage. The dynamic storage area is divided into two regions. One part is used to store objects and when the size of the remaining area in the object storage region becomes less than a certain threshold value, then active objects in the current object storage

region are copied into the second object storage region. Then the two object storage regions change their roles each other.

4. EVALUATION OF THE VFP SYSTEM

In this section we discuss the feasibility of the vector processing approach in implementation of the FP-like functional programming languages. We carry out performance evaluation of the VFP system in three levels, namely 1) in primitive function level, 2) in functional form level and 3) in program function level. We give timing results of our VFP system on FACOM VP-200 at Data Processing Center of Kyoto University.

4.1 The Effect of Vector Operation in Primitive Functions

Timing results of 'distl' and 'trans' as examples of sequence-transformation functions and that of 'iota' are given in the following Tables.

Table 1 CPU Time of 'distl' in milliseconds

length	scalar	vector
100	0.114	0.043
600	0.648	0.187

Table 2 CPU Time of 'trans' in milliseconds.

length	scalar	vector
600	1.868	1.439

Table 3 CPU Time of 'iota' in milliseconds

length	scalar	vector
100	0.045	0.013
600	0.283	0.023

In case of 'distl' or 'trans' operation, the input object is a sequence and the sequence is represented by a sequence of pointers to element objects. The operation involves the indirect vector accessing (normally called as list-vector access) and its performance depends on the characteristic of the vectorcomputer used. It is natural that the longer is the length of sequence, higher is the computation speed ratio of the vector mode over the scalar mode. In case of 'iota' function, the input is a single integer and the output object can be formed without using indirect access and the effect of vector operation is comparatively large.

4.2 The effect of Vector Operation in Functional Form Operation

We give results of some examples involving 'apply-to-all' operations and 'insertion' operations.

Table 4 CPU Time of '/ +' in milliseconds

length	scalar	vector
100	0.046	0.010
600	0.249	0.013

Table 5 CPU Time of 'α +' in milliseconds

length	scalar	vector
100	0.294	0.037
600	1.761	0.078

4.3 The Effect of Vector Operation in Program Level Functions

Table 6 CPU Time of 'α ÷' in milliseconds

length	scalar	vector
100	0.406	0.048
600	2.411	0.105

We give timing results for three examples:

1) Inner Product

The timing result of the inner product program is given in the following table:

Table 7 CPU Time of {IP ≡ / + ∘ α * ∘ trans} in milliseconds

Table 7 CPU Time of {IP ≡ / + ∘ α * ∘ trans} in milliseconds

length	scalar	vector
100	0.662	0.297
600	3.896	1.519

The effect of the vector operation in 'trans' function is not large, therefore the effect of the total program is only about two even when the number of elements in data vectors is 600.

2) Prime Number Generator

The following FP program to compute prime numbers was used.

```
{prime ≡ p ∘ tl ∘ iota}
{p ≡ (eq0 ∘ length ->[ ];
    apndl ∘ [first, p ∘ q ∘ distr ∘ [tl, first]])}
{q  ≡ concat ∘  α (eq0 ∘ mod -> [ ];[first])}
{eq0  ≡ eq ∘ [id, 0]}
```

Table 8 gives CPU timing results of the program 'prime' in milliseconds.

Table 8 CPU Time of the program
'prime' in milliseconds

length	scalar	vector
100	10.230	9.843
600	136.302	96.484

3) Eight Queens Problem

We show a FP program for the eight Queens problem and its timing result. Derivation of this program is given in the reference[3].

{Queen ≡ / j ∘ apndr ∘ [α 1 ∘ distl ∘ [id, iota ∘ sub1], i]}

{j ≡ checkl ∘ addqueen}

{i ≡ α [id] ∘ iota}

{addqueen ≡ concat ∘ α (α apndr) ∘ α distl ∘ distr
    ∘ [2, iota ∘ 1]}

{checkl ≡ drop ∘ [α check, id]}

{check ≡ (colcheck -> T̄; digcheck)}

{colcheck ≡ / or ∘ α eq ∘ distr ∘ [tlr, last]}

{digcheck ≡ / or ∘ α eq ∘ trans ∘ [α (abs ∘ -)
    ∘ distr ∘ [tlr, last],reverse ∘ iota ∘ sub1 ∘ length]}

{eq1 ≡ eq ∘ [id, 1]}

{sub1 ≡ - ∘ [id, 1]}

{abs ≡ (gt ∘ [id, ō] -> id; - ∘ [ō, id])}

Table 9 CPU Time of the program 'n-Queen'
for n = 8 in seconds

	scalar	vector
cputime	2.936s	1.820s
vector unittime		0.72s

It should be noted the CPU time needed to compute the solution of the eight Queens problem by the above FP program by the Berkeley FP system on VAX-780 is more than 909 seconds.

5 CONCLUSION

We described the method to make use of the vector processing facility in implementation of the FP-like functional programming languages. In our VFP system, data structures suitable for vector processing are adopted, and parallel type primitive functions such as 'distl','distr' or parallel type functional forms such as 'apply-to-all' can be efficiently interpreted. We also showed the method to improve the vectorization ratio which is crucial to attain high performance on vectorcomputers. The timing results on FACOM VP-200 shows that current vectorcomputers are mainly designed for floating-point computations but that it is possible to attain certain level of speed-up in implementation of the FP-like languages.

Acknowledgments

Mr. T. Kenjou, a student of our group joined in the early stage of implementation of the VFP system and contributed to program development.

REFERENCES

1. Backus, J.: Can Programming Be Liberated from the von Neumann Style? A Functional Style and its Algebra of Programs, C.ACM vol.21, pp.613-641, 1978.

2. Scott, B.: Berkeley FP User's Manual, Rev 4.1, 1981.

3. Shimasaki, M.: Program Derivation and Transformation in FP . submitted for publication.

Compiling Optimizations through Program Transformations

Michiaki Yasumura
Central Research Lab., Hitachi Ltd.
Kokubunji, Tokyo 185
Japan

ABSTRACT

The purpose of this research is to add the program transformation methods into the repertoire of optimizing compilers. Precisely speaking, it asserts that the vectorization is in fact a program transformation, that the vectorization can be enhanced by introducing program transformations, such as partial vectorization and loop expansions, etc., and that an optimizing compiler for Common Lisp can also be enhanced by introducing program transformations, such as self-inline expansion. Meanwhile, the algorithms such as the partial vectorization algorithm and the breadth-first data flow analysis have been developed.

1. INTRODUCTION

1.1 Purpose of the Study

Research on optimizing compiler, which optimize the object code they generate, started simultaneously with the development of the first compiler. The optimization of loops has been widely studied, especially for FORTRAN compilers. Optimization techniques concentrated on removal of unnecessary operations, such as common expression elimination and redundant operation removal.

Recently, vector compilers for super-computers and vector processors have been developed, and they are categorized as optimizing compilers. Though there are some studies on basic algorithms for vector compilers, most effort is devoted to developing practical compilers, and few studies report on systematic research into techniques for vector compilers.

On the other hand, the research on program transformations, such as the study by Darlington, Burstall of Edinburgh University, have become popular. At first, studies on program transformation were mainly for functional programming languages, but recently research on program transformation for logic programming languages has appeared. This research is theoretical rather than practical.

In this thesis, it is aimed to introduce the concept of program transformation into the field of optimizing compilation, to substantiate the program transformation in the practical area, and to develope a new step in optimizing compilation.

More precisely speaking, it is intended to recognize vectorization as a program transformation, to extend vectorization by introducing several program transformation techniques, and to achieve high-performance object code by introducing program transformation into an actual language.

1.2 Program Transformation and Optimization

Optimizing compilation is a process which maximises the efficiency of object code during the object generation phase of a compiler. Literally, optimization means the generated code is the most efficient possible, but it is usually difficult to realize a complete optimization. Therefore, it is correctly called 'improvement', but here we use optimization in accordance with conventional terminology.

Optimization includes local optimization, such as peephole optimization, which optimizes code only by local information; global optimization, which optimizes code by analyzing global data flow of variables; and register optimization, which allocates registers effectively.

Each of them improves code by transforming the object or intermediate forms and therefore they are similar to program transformation.

Program transformation☆ is a transformation from source to source, or a transformation which changes program structure. Optimization, on the other hand, is a transformation of intermediate code and it changes program structure little. Program transformation evolves from the stage of transformation by hand, to the stage of axiomatization, and finally the stage of automatic transformation. In this thesis, program transformation, including automatic transformation, is studied.

A program transformation T is a transformation of program P into P' which leaves Ip, the meaning of program P, and Ip', the meaning of program P', equivalent :

$$T: P \rightarrow P' \text{ and } \text{Ip} \simeq \text{Ip'}$$

For the program transformation $T : P \rightarrow P'$, let the efficiency of program P be Ep and the efficiency of program P' be Ep'. Then the purpose of program transformation $T : P \rightarrow P'$ is that $Ep \leq Ep'$ should hold true, that is to say, the efficiency of transformed program should be equal to or better than that of the original program.

The program semantics should be rigorously defined as follows :

The program semantics Ip of a program P is that the set of output variables O obtained by the set of input variables I for the program P. And therefore if the set of output variables O' obtained by the same set of input variables I for the program P' is equal to O, $\text{Ip} \simeq \text{Ip'}$ must hold good.

Here, the efficiency of a program Ep is represented by the execution speed (the inverse of execution time) of the program. For example, MFLOPS (Million Floating Operation Per Second) is a unit of the efficiency of a program for numeric calculations. The vectorization ratio (the ratio of the time of vectorizable part over total execution time) or the ratio of parallelization could be another candidate.

-------- (note) ----------------------
☆When we consider program transformation, P and P' must be the same language. Therefore we do not call the transformation from source to object, 'program transformation'.

One of the earliest researches on program transformations was done by Darlington and Burstall of Univ. of Edinburgh[4], [6]. They showed a transformation method of a functional language which applys rules of unfolding, folding, abstraction, and instatiation with recursive equations. But their method is not always suitable to automatic transformation.

On the other hand, several transformation methods which transform recursive calls into iterative form were proposed. Among them, the transformation of tail recursion into an iterative loop is well known, and has been adapted by many modern Lisp compilers. Also, several people noticed that if the tail function holds to the associative law then it can be also transformed into iterative form.

Little research treats vectorization as a kind of program transformation (we elaborate in next sub-chapter). One exception is the work done by Loveman, who showed source program transformation methods for Illiac IV Fortran compiler [18].

1.3 Vectorization

Here, vectorization, which is the primary concept of vector compilers, is described.

In Fortran programs, it is empirically known that the most of the total execution time is consumed by DO loops such as the one in Fig. 1.1 [13]. In the scalar processing mode, one operation is executed for each index value. After all operations in a DO loop are executed for an index value, the index value is incremented, and each operation is executed again for the new index value, and so on. In the vector processing mode, each operation is executed for all index values, and the next operation is executed for all index values, and so on. This change in execution order is called loop distribution or vectorization (Fig. 1.1)

This vectorization is a kind of transformation of programs, and it is correctly called program transformation when the program semantics remain unchanged after the transformation. In vector compilers, the vectorization is the most fundamental transformation, and is therefore called the principal transformation.

```
FORTRAN DO loop          Vector mode
   DO 10 i=1,N
   A(i)=B(i)+C(i)   => (Aᵢ=Bᵢ+Cᵢ, i=1,N)
10 D(i)=A(i)*E(i)      (Dᵢ=Aᵢ*Eᵢ, i=1,N)
```

Fig. 1.1 Loop distribution (Vectorization)

In order to treat vectorization as a program transformation, the program semantics must be kept unchanged, that is to say, the program's results must be the same despite the transformation. For this assurance, the data dependency, the relation of variable definitions and references, must be verified to be unchanged. This is called the analysis of data dependency.

Data dependency is classified into five categories:
① suitably dependent
② unsuitably dependent
③ specially dependent
④ unknown dependent
⑤ independent

It is called suitably dependent when the results of the program are unchanged after the change of execution order by vectorization. It is called unsuitably dependent when it is not suitably dependent. Fig. 1.2 shows examples of unsuitably dependent loops. In DO10, the variable S is unsuitably dependent, and in DO20 the array A is unsuitably dependent.

Suitably dependent is a special case of unsuitably dependent, and these specially dependent operations are vectorized by special hardware support. Therefore, a specially dependent operation is also called a special operation. Table1.1 shows examples of specially dependent cases.

Our basic dependency analysis is done for variables and for arrays according to the following rules:

(1) A variable is unsuitably dependent if there is a defining occurrence and its first occurrence is not a defining occurrence.

(2) An array is unsuitably dependent if one of the two occurrences is a defining occurrence and the preceding occurrence contains a subscript, the

```
        DO 10 I=1,N
        A(I)=S*B(I)
        S=C(I)+D(I)
    10 continue


        DO 20 I=1,N
        A(I-1)=B(I)*C(I)
        D(I)=A(I)+E(I)
    20 continue
```

Fig. 1.2 Examples of unsuitably dependent loops.

Table 1.1 Specially dependent case

special operation	example
Vector Sum	$S = S + A(i)$
Vector Product	$S = S*A(i)$
Inner Product	$S = S + A(i)*B(i)$
Vector Iteration	$A(i + 1) = A(i)*B(i) + C(i)$
Vector Max	$S = MAX(S,A(i))$
Vector Min	$S = MIN(S,A(i))$

value of which is "less than" (☆) the value of the subscript of the succeeding occurrence. For the detail of subscript analysis, see [31].

(☆) The value of subscript F_i is "less than"
the value of subscript F_j iff

$\exists\, p,q(1 \le p < q \le n)\ f_i q = f_j p$

where $F_i = (f_i 1, f_i 2, \ldots, f_i n)$ and $F_j = (f_j 1, f_j 2, \ldots, f_j n)$
are ordered set of subscript values.

1.4 Summary and Discussions

In this chapter, the relation of optimizing compilation to program transformation, and an overview of the earlier works on program transformation, are described. The method of data dependency analysis, which is the basic algorithm of vector compilers, is also described. This algorithm is based primary on [31]. A vector compiler based on this algorithm has been developed for the M180 IAP (Integrated Array Processor), and is the first automatic vector compiler in Japan. This chapter is the basis for chapter 2 and 3.

1.5 Organization of the Paper

In chapter 1, the purpose of the paper and the subjects of the study, which are optimizing compilation and program transformation, are stated. Among them, the data dependency analysis, which is the basic algorithm of vectorization, is described thoroughly.

In chapter 2, a partial vectorization algorithm by loop splitting, which separates vectorizable parts of a loop from the unvectorizable part, is described.

In chapter 3, an extended vectorization algorithm, involving a statement exchange algorithm and a condition statement vectorization algorithm, is described. It is based on the basic vectorization algorithm described in chapter 1, and which includes the partial vectorization algorithm stated in chapter 2

In chapter 4, optimization algorithms for Lisp optimizing compilers, mainly program transformation algorithms such as self inline expansion are described.

In chapter 5, implementations and performance evaluations for the loop splitting, the extended vectorization and the Lisp compiler optimization are described.

2. PARTIAL VECTORIZATION BY LOOP SPLITTING

2.1 Automatic Loop Splitting

Automatic vector compilers have usually vectorized programs without trying to rewrite the source code, and DO loops which contained any unvectorizable factor became unvectorizable. Therefore, when a DO loop contained some vectorizable parts, it had to be split by hand. But rewriting by hand is tedious work, and runs the risk of incurring new errors. In automatic vector compilers it is hoped to automatically partially vectorize DO loops by extracting vectorizable parts from the unvectorizable parts. Fig. 2.1 shows an example of partial vectorization by loop splitting. In this example, it is assumed that built-in function FLOAT is unvectorizable.☆

```
                          DO 10 I=1,N
     DO 10 I=1,N            A(I)=FLOAT(I)
     A(I)=FLOAT(I)       10 CONTINUE
     C(I)=A(I)*B(I)  =>     DO 11 I=1,N
  10 CONTINUE   splitting   C(I)=A(I)*B(I)
                         11 CONTINUE
```

Fig. 2.1 An example of partial vectorization by loop splitting.

In Fig. 2.1, before the loop splitting the whole DO loop is unvectorizable, but after the loop splitting the second DO loop is vectorizable, though the first one remains unvectorizable.

Not every DO loop is a candidate for loop splitting. Table 2.1 shows examples of totally unvectorizable DO loops. DO loops other than these totally unvectorizable DO loops are candidates for loop splitting. Table 2.2 shows an example of partially unvectorizable factors. Factors shown in table 2.2 are partialized as unvectorizable parts by loop splitting. Unvectorizable factors shown in table 2.1 and table 2.2 are just examples, and they can

-------- (note) -----------------------

☆ Float is just an example; the exact list of unvectorizable operations depends on the hardware.

change depending on the instruction repertoires and on the state of the art or the support domain of vector compilers.

Table 2.1 Examples of totally unvectorizable DO loops.

---

(1) loops with a jump to outside the loop
(2) loops with subprogram calls

Table 2.2 Example of partially unvectorizable factors.

---

(1) inner cyclic loop, backward jump
(2) data dependency unsuitable
(3) unsupported statements (e.g. I/O statement)
(4) unsupported types (e.g. character type)
(5) unsupported built-in functions

2.2 Principles of Loop Splitting

There are three basic principles of loop splitting:

(1) make vectorizable parts as large as possible

(2) minimize the added overhead of new loops

(3) ensure the correctness of program transformation.

Item (1) is the main purpose of loop splitting, that is to say, to make as much of the program as possible benefit from the vectorization speed-up. Item (2) means that unvectorizable parts contain overhead, such as loop control, and that it is not desirable to have many small unvectorizable parts. In general, the requirement (2) conflicts with the requirement (1). Therefore, the proper size of splitting grain must be determined by balancing (1) and (2). In this study, we determined that the smallest unit of splitting would be the statement, and did not consider splitting within statements. Beyond that, inter-statement splitting would be as small as possible. Conditional statements are left unsplit. Finally, unnecessary splitting, such as splitting within a vectorizable or unvectorizable part, would be avoided.

In order to preserve correctness of program transformation by loop splitting, the data dependency analysis mentioned in chapter 1 must be performed. The data dependency of a variable or an array over the split point must be suitable, but the data dependency within a unvectorizable part may be unsuitable.

Also if a variable is defined before the split point and referred to after the split point, it is necessary to promote it into an array to pass the values over the split point (Fig. 2.2).

```
                                DO 10 I=1,N
      DO 10 I=1,N                 S(I)=FLOAT(I)
      S=FLOAT(I)              10 CONTINUE
      A(I)=B(I)*S    =>         DO 11 I=1,N
  10 CONTINUE                     A(I)=B(I)*S(I)
                             11 CONTINUE
                                S=S(N)
```

Fig. 2.2 The promotion of a variable to an array for loop splitting.

When a forward jump points to a split point, the corresponding statement number must be modified (Fig. 2.3).

```
                                DO 10 I=1,N
      DO 10 I=1,N                 IF(J.EQ.M) GOTO 110
      IF(J.EQ.M) GOTO 100         A(I)=FLOAT(I)
      A(I)=FLOAT(I)   =>     110 CONTINUE
  100 C(I)=A(I)*B(I)          10 CONTINUE
   10 CONTINUE                  DO 11 I=1,N
                            100 C(I)=A(I)*B(I)
                             11 CONTINUE
```

Fig. 2.3 Alteration of the statement number at the split point.

As the results of the above considerations, the principles of loop splitting are as follows:

(1)   Let innermost DO loops, other than the loops shown in table 2.1, be the candidates for loop splitting, and partialize unvectorizable parts by detecting unvectorizable factors shown in table 2.2.

(2)   Do not split inside a conditional statement. Split statementwise in other cases.

(3)   If a variable is referenced across the split point, promote it into an array.

(4)   Make sure the data dependency across the split point is correct.

(5)   Modify the branch destinations of forward jumps to the split point.

(6)   Combine vectorizable parts together and unvectorizable parts together.

2.3 Method of Loop Splitting

Based on the principles of loop splitting described in the previous section, the process of loop splitting is done with the following steps:

(1)   [Detection of split candidates] Merge unvectorizable parts as much as possible, and split vectorizable parts as little as possible, then detect split candidate points.

(2)   [Adjustment of split candidates] Combine and merge the parts to be split (called S-Block) by analyzing data dependency.

(3)   [Promotion of variable into array] Promote the variables that are laid across split points into arrays.

(4)   [Generation of split object] Determine split points, modify branch statements, alterate intermediate codes and internal tables.

The following sections describe the details of the implementation of each step in an automatic vector compiler.

2.3.1 Detection of loop split candidates

Before detecting loop split candidates, control flow analysis must be done. The control flow inside a loop is represented by a directed graph (program flow diagram) which consists of vertices (blocks) and directed edges. A vertex is a collection of statements in which there is no control

transition. Figure 2.4 shows an example of a directed graph. Directed graphs used for vector compilers are almost the same as those used for optimizing compilers, but there are few minor differences☆.

For the directed graphs, a vertex through which every path from the start point to the end point goes is called articulation point, and any other vertex is called non-articulation point. In Fig. 2.4, a grey circle denotes an articulation point, whereas a white one denotes a non-articulation point.

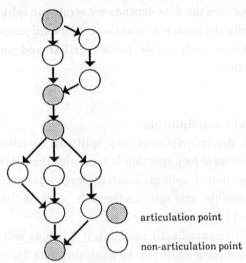

articulation point

non-articulation point

Fig. 2.4   An example of the directed graph.

After making a directed graph, articulation points are determined and cycles (small inner loops) are detected. This control flow analysis [41] is based on depth-first-traversal method and is remedied by applying if-then-else-reduction (Fig. 2.5).

Using the information of directed graphs and articulation points, non-articulation points and their controlling articulation point (the conditional statement as a whole) become candidate unit for splitting, and any other

-------- (note) -----------------------
☆Compared with directed graphs for optimization, directed graphs for vector compilers not only represent control flows but also assume statements as basic components of vertexes (blocks).

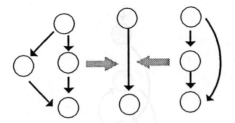

Fig. 2.5   If-then-else reduction.

articulation point (i.e. a non-conditional statement) becomes another candidate unit for splitting. These candidate are called S-Blocks. For each S-Block, vectorization marks are set according to the table 2.2, as follows:

(1)   S-Blocks which constitute a cycle are unvectorizable.

(2)   S-Blocks which constitute a cycle-free backward jump are also unvectorizable (Fig. 2.6), since the control flow is inconsistent with the sequential program text.

(3)   S-Blocks which contain built-in functions, data types, or statements that are not supported by the vector hardware.

(4)   A sequence of unvectorizable S-Blocks is merged into a single S-Block.

By this method, the points between the S-Block become candidate loop split points. Note that a vectorizable S-Block may now be adjacent to another vectorizable S-Block, but no unvectorizable S-Block will be adjacent to another unvectorizable S-Block.

2.3.2 Adjustment of split point candidates

Adjustment of split point candidates is done in parallel with the data dependency analysis, and as the result of it the integration of S-Blocks is performed. The data dependency analysis is done for (1)variables, (2) arrays and (3) special operations, in that order.

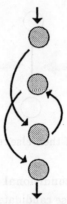

Fig. 2.6   An example of cycle-free backward jump

(1) The data dependency analysis for a variable is performed throughout a DO loop. If the loop contains a definition of the variable's value, it checks whether the first occurrence is the definition or not. If the first definition appears inside a conditional statement, this check must be extended. If the data dependency of the variable is suitable, and its definition and the reference appear in different S-Blocks, the variable is flagged as potentially . If the data dependency of the variable is unsuitable, the sequence of S-Blocks beginning with the S-Block which contains the first occurrence of the variable, and ending with the S-Block which contains the last occurrence, become unsuitablly dependent.

(2) The data dependency analysis for an array is performed to check data dependency by "comparing subscripts"☆ of pair of occurrences. If they are unsuitably dependent, then the S-Block containing both occurrences, plus all S-Blocks in between, become unvectorizable, and are merged with adjacent unvectorizable S-Blocks (if any).

-------- (note) -----------------------

☆ The comparison of subscripts is done by the subscript structure with initial expression, incremental expression and final expression. If the result of the comparison is unknown, it is treated as a unsuitable dependent case.

(3) The data dependency analysis for special operations performed by checking the data dependency within a single unvectorizable statement (therefore within a single S-Block). And if it is determined as unsuitable, then the S-Block becomes unvectorizable, and is merged with adjacent unvectorizable S-Blocks (if any).

Figure 2.7 shows an example of the data dependency analysis and integration of S-Blocks. In the figure, the data dependency of array A is being checked when S_i, S_j, S_k, S_l are vectorizable and S_m is unvectorizable. Since the defining occurrence of array element A(i-1) in S_j is unsuitable to the array element A(i) in S_l, S_j and S_l must be merged together. In this case S_k, which lies between S_j and S_l and its contiguous unvectorizable S-Block Sm should be merged together. As the result, the detection of unsuitability of S_j and S_l yields the integration of S-Block from S_j through S_m.

After the data dependency analysis within a vectorizable S-Block and among different S-Blocks, the data dependency for both vectorization and loop splitting is guaranteed. At this point, no two unvectorizable S-Blocks are adjacent, but vectorizable S-Blocks may be.

After the data dependency analysis,

(4) Sequence of vectorizable S-Blocks are integrated.

(5) Useless vectorizable S-Blocks, such as those which contain only CONTINUE statements, are removed.

If after the integration of the S-Blocks, a DO loop becomes a single vectorizable or unvectorizable S-Block, then loop splitting should not be performed.

If vectorizable S-Blocks and unvectorizable S-Blocks remain, their borders become loop split points.

2.3.3 Promotion of variables into arrays

While adjusting of split point candidates, potentially promoted variables were flagged. After the establishment of loop split points, the flag is canceled for variables which appear in only one S-Block. Therefore when the split points are fixed, the promoted variables are also fixed. The fixed promoted variables are processed to be converted into arrays, as follows:

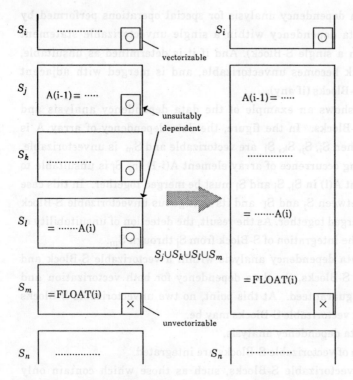

Fig. 2.7 An example of data reference check and S-Block integration .

(1) Create new dictionary table for new arrays☆.

(2) Modify intermediate codes for promoted variables into codes for new arrays.

(3) Create a new index variable (if necessary) for new arrays, and insert intermediate codes for initialization and for updates of the index variable.

(4) Insert intermediate codes for final value of the promoted variables just after the DO loop.

-------- (note) ------------------------

☆ Array size is determined by loop length or the declaration for the arrays which appears in the loop. If both of them are unknown, then user option determines.

2.3.4 Generation of split object

For each loop split point, intermediate codes, statement number, and control informations are updated as follows:

(1) Modify forward jumps aimed at the split point.

As the figure 2.3 shows, if a loop contains the forward jump to the split point, a new statement number is created just before the split point, and the intermediate codes and control informations are modified so that the branch to the split point is modified to the jump to the new statement number. Backward jumps remain as they are.

(2) Create new statement number for the loop split point.

If the split point is in the sequence of simple assignment statements, a new statement number is created for it, and corresponding control informations are changed.

(3) Insert intermediate codes for updating index variables.

Intermediate codes for updating index variables, which are used within each S-Block, are inserted at the tail (or at the head, according to the type of index variables) of each S-Block.

(4) Generate intermediate codes for branch.

Intermediate codes for a branch to the header statement number of each S-Block is generated at the tail of the S-Block. At that time, intermediate codes for updating loop control variable are also added. The control information is modified.

(5) Insert intermediate codes for initializing index variables.

Intermediate codes for initializing index variables which are used within each S-Block are inserted just before the split point.

(6) Insert intermediate codes for setting finale values to new index variables.

Intermediate codes for setting finale values to new index variables are inserted just after the loop.

In the above process, the header S-Block and the tail S-Block are treated differently with intermediate S-Blocks☆.

-------- (note) -----------------------

☆For example, the tail S-Block does not need the insertion of the intermediate codes for branch.

2.4 Summary and Discussions

This chapter described the details of the partial vectorization method by loop splitting which separates vectorizable parts from unvectorizable parts in the DO loops that contain unvectorizable factors. A data dependency analysis algorithm is used for determining loop splitting. Variables which are referenced across a split point are promoted into arrays, because promoted variables must be compatible both for vectorizable and unvectorizable parts, although they become temporary vectors if they appear only in a vectorizable part, or they remain as variables if they appear only in a unvectorizable part. The grain of loop splitting is statementwise, since the target vector processor is IAP, in which the performance ratio of scalar and vector is not so high, and the overhead yielded by loop splitting must be considered. It is easily extended the algorithm to split statement into expression-wise, and the extension is preferred to super-computers. Actually the vector compiler for S-810 performs expression-wise splitting based on the algorithm.

When the referenced paper [42] of this thesis appeared, the vector compiler (M200H/M280H IAP compiler) based on that algorithm was the only vector compiler which performed automatic loop splitting. Since then, other vector compilers have been appeared which also do loop splitting.

3. EXTENSIONS TO THE DATA DEPENDENCY ANALYSIS

3.1 Extension to the Basic Vectorization

The vectorization analysis is based on this basic algorithm [31] and is enhanced by some program transformation techniques. At least three program transformation techniques are related to the data dependency analysis:

①statement exchanging
② loop splitting
③loop unrolling for a cyclic index.

During the data dependency analysis, if two statements are exchangeable, they are exchanged to reduce unsuitable dependency.

Two statements are exchangeable iff

variables/arrays in two statements are mutually unsuitably dependent or independent, but are neither suitably dependent nor unknown.

In the course of the data dependency analysis, a loop is split into vectorizable parts and unvectorizable parts.

The loop splitting algorithm is as follows:

(1) Let an assignment statement or a conditional statement be a S-Block (Split-Block).

(2) Analyze the data dependencies within a vectorizable S-Block and among S-Blocks, and mark the S-Block unvectorizable if it contains unsuitably dependent or unknown dependent variables/arrays.

(3) Combine adjacent unvectorizable S-Blocks. Repeat step 2 until all S-Blocks are checked.

(4) Combine adjacent vectorizable S-Blocks.

The resultant S-Block is quite similar to the PI-Block produced by the data dependency graph [15].

Data dependency analysis is effective only for linear indexes. Data dependency analysis for non-linear indexes, such as indirect addressing is quite difficult. Therefore, an array with a non-linear index can only be

vectorized if its occurrences are use-only or it appears only once. Otherwise it should be declared independent by the user (Fig. 3.1).

```
*VOPTION VEC
      DO 10 i=1,N
      A(L(i))=A(L(i))+B(i)
   10 CONTINUE
```

Fig. 3.1 User-Declared Vectorization

A cyclic index is a non-linear index. A program with a cyclic index, however, can be vectorized through a loop unrolling technique. In Fig. 3.2 cyclic index j is removed by loop unrolling.

```
 Original loop          Unrolled loop
    j=N                  A(1)=B(N)+C(1)
    DO 10 i=1,N          DO 10 i=2,N
    A(i)=B(j)+C(i)   =>  A(i)=B(i-1)+C(i)
 10 j=i              10 CONTINUE
```

Fig. 3.2 Loop Unrolling for a Cyclic Index

3.2 Vectorizing IF Statements

To vectorize IF statements, control flow and data flow (data dependency under IF statements) are first analyzed.

The main purposes of control flow analysis are to detect anomalies, such as internal loops or branches into control structures (see Fig. 3.3), and clarify control and controlled relationships.

Control flow analysis is relatively easy and little is new to vector compilers.

The situation is different for data flow analysis. Data dependency of arrays within IF statements is the same as that without IF statements.

129

```
          DO 10 i=1,N
          IF(e1) GOTO 2
     1      s1
          GOTO 3
     2  IF(e2) THEN
            s2
          ELSE
            s3
          GOTO 1
          END IF
     3    s4
    10 CONTINUE
```

Fig. 3.3 An Anomalous Control Structure

However data dependency of variables with IF statements is different (Fig. 3.4).

```
Case A:  IF(  ) THEN
            S=...
         ELSE
            ..=S
         ENDIF
         ...=S

Case B:  IF(  ) THEN
            S=...
         ELSE
            S=...
         ENDIF
         ...=S

Case C:  IF(  ) THEN
            S=...
            ..=S
         ELSE
            ...
         ENDIF
```

Fig. 3.4 Data Dependency Under IF

Case A is unvectorizable, even though the definition of variable S precedes its use textually. Case B is vectorizable, since the variable is totally defined and both definitions precede its use. Case C is vectorizable, though the variable is only partially defined. Here, a variable is totally defined if its defining occurrence appears on every path of the flow graph. Otherwise, it is called partially defined.

Thus the data dependency condition is modified as follows:

(1)' A variable is unsuitably dependent if there is a defining occurrence and there is a path on which the defining occurrence does not precede the other occurrence.

To check the above condition in the IAP compiler, the depth-first traverse approach was attempted at first. This method is simple and there is no extra memory except for backtracking. However, it was too slow to analyze a fairly large DO loop with many IF statements. Therefore we introduced an if-then-else reduction method, which reduces if-then or if-then-else branches and makes the depth-first method practical. (Note: if-then-reduction method was described in chapter 2). Nevertheless, the depth-first method is an intrinsically time-consuming process.

So we have developed the breadth-first data flow method for the S-810 compiler. To facilitate this method we have introduced the data flow operators, $\cap^*$ and $\cup^*$.

For each variable v and each index i in a flow graph, there are three data flow variables $IN_i(v)$, $OWN_i(v)$, $OUT_i(v)$ defined as follows:

$$IN_i(v) = \underset{j \in Pred(i)}{\cap^*} OUT_j(v)$$

$$OWN_i(v) = \begin{cases} -1 & \text{(use precedes)} \\ 0 & \text{(not appear)} \\ +1 & \text{(def precedes)} \end{cases}$$

$$OUT_i(v) = IN_i \cup^* OWN_i(v)$$

Here, $IN_i(v)$ is the input status for the variable v in vertex i, $OWN_i(v)$ is the own status for the variable v in vertex i, and $OUT_i(v)$ is the output status for the variable v in vertex i.

The semantics of $\cap^*$ and $\cup^*$ are defined in Table 3.1. The **value -1 is** interpreted as the unsuitably dependent state, whereas the value 1 is the suitably dependent state. The initial state of each variable is set to 0, the neutral state.

Table 3.1. Data flow operators.

```
       ∩*                              ∪*
                                       OWN
+----+-----------+       +----+-----------+
|    | -1  0 +1  |       |    | -1  0 +1  |
+----+-----------+       +----+-----------+
| -1 | -1 -1 -1  |    IN| -1 | -1 -1 -1  |
|  0 | -1  0  0  |      | 0  | -1  0 +1  |
| +1 | -1  0 +1  |      | +1 | +1 +1 +1  |
+----+-----------+       +----+-----------+
```

Unary $\cap^*$ is defined by binary $\cap^*$ as follows:

$$\cap^*_{j=1..n} X_j = X_1 \cap^* X_2 \cap^* \ldots \cap^* X_n$$

Using these operators and status variables, the flow graph is traversed in breadth-first order. If the value OUT of the final vertex is not -1, then it is suitably dependent or independent. (See the example in Fig. 3.5)

This algorithm is efficient in the sense that each vertex is traversed only once. In general this algorithm is quite useful for various data dependency of variables, such as variables under nested IF statements or partially defined variables.

Vectorization of IF statements can be further extended based on the above algorithm. For example, if semantics analysis is employed, some special cases can be vectorized as well. Such an example is shown in Fig. 3.6.

This example is an unsuitably dependent case by definition, since there is a definition of a variable and there is a path on which there is no preceding definition of the usage. However, when the semantics of IF statement are considered, this IF expression is index-independent (we call this type of IF statement loop invariant IF statement). Therefore this definition of the variable is either always or never executed, for all index values, and so can be vectorized.

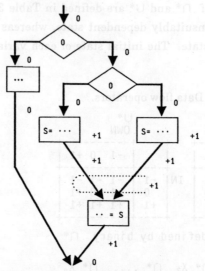

Fig. 3.5 An example of the data flow analysis

```
         DO 10 i=1,N
         IF(A(K).EQ.X) S=B(I)
         C(I)=S*D(I)
      10 CONTINUE
```

Fig. 3.6 An example of semantics analysis of an IF statement

The other technique for enhancing vectorization of IF statements is related to the program transformation techniques. One example is the loop unrolling of edge conditions. In Fig. 3.7, the IF statement of an edge condition is removed by loop unrolling.

3.3 Summary and Discussions

This chapter describes extensions to the basic data dependency analysis described in chapter 1 by adding the loop splitting algorithm described in chapter 2 and two new extensions, statement exchanges and vectorization of control statements.

```
   DO 10 i=1,N
   IF(i.EQ.1) THEN          A(1)=0.0
      A(i)=0.0              DO 10 i=2,N
   ELSE           =>           A(i)=S*B(i)
      A(i)=S*B(i)        10 CONTINUE
   END IF
10 CONTINUE
```

Fig. 3.7 An example of loop unrolling for an edge condition

This algorithms were applied to the vector compiler for the S-810 supercomputer, and proved their effectiveness (see §5.2). Vectorization of conditional statements was first implemented in the IAP compiler for M280H. The detail of the vectorization algorithm for conditional statements is described in 38), 9). In this chapter, an extended principle for data dependency analysis and breadth-first data dependency analysis method by introducing data flow operators are newly described.

The data dependency analysis by Kuck, et.al 15) is a method in which data dependencies are classified into data dependent (definition precedes reference), anti-dependent (reference precedes definition) and output-dependent (sequence of definition), where these relations are represented as a graph (called the dependency graph) to be manipulated for vectorization. The manipulation of the graph would seem to be easy, but the details of the dependency analysis, such as array subscript analysis, are unknown, which makes comparison with our algorithm impossible. Theoretically, the results of vectorization with our methods and those with their dependency graph should be almost the same. They also classify control dependencies as conditional statements, but the results of the vectorization of conditional statements with this classification are unknown.

4. PROGRAM TRANSFORMATION FOR A LISP COMPILER

4.1 Background

More than twenty-five years have past since the emergence of Lisp, and meanwhile many Lisp dialects and their language processors have been developed. Recently a language specification for Common Lisp has appeared which compromises the specifications of main dialects 30).

Common Lisp contains many features of older Lisps, and it also has the function as a first class object, in a way that adapts lexical scope rules, full closures, and multiple values. It also has many capabilities such as extended data types (e.g. structures), generic functions for sequences☆ and numbers, and extended input/output (e.g. format), and these features are useful for many applications, especially for A.I. applications. With these rich capabilities it is assumed to be difficult to implement an efficient language processor.

On the other hand, many Lisp users have complained of their processors slow execution speed, lack of capabilities and compatibilities, limitation of memory size, incomplete Japanese language facilities, and so on 22). Among these complaints, execution speed is the most crucial.

We consider the Lisp language a basic tool for A.I. researches in our laboratory, and have implemented a Lisp processor called HiLISP (High performance Lisp), and its compiler which are aimed at solving the above problems. The HiLISP compiler is a one of the utilities of the HiLISP system, but is the most important one in the sense that it must generate high-speed object codes.

This chapter describes the design philosophy of HiLISP system (which forms the premise for the HiLISP compiler), the design methodology of HiLISP compiler, and implemetation method and optimization algorithms for the compiler.

-------- (note) ----------------------
☆ Common structure for lists and for one-dimensional vectors.

4.2 Design Philosophy

Requirements for the HiLISP system, which runs on a mainframe computer, are summarized as follows:

(1) Runs efficiently – Attention is paid for how much speed can be attained on stock hardware, how much quicker (or slower) it is than the conventional languages, such as Pascal or C, and how its the performance compares with older Lisp specifications.

(2) Complies with Common Lisp – The language specification complies with Common Lisp, which has sufficient power and is oriented toward the Lisp standard.

(3) Supports Japanese characters fully – Japanese characters and strings can be used not only as comments or data but also as symbol names.

(4) Has friendly support environments – Full-screen structure editor and full debugger are provided.

(5) Provides large memory space – Older Lisp processors on main frame computers allows not more than 16MB memory, but it is necessary to allow approximately 2GB memory for the newer Lisp processor.

(6) Also – Interfaces to other languages and to the Operating System are required.

In addition to above mentioned requirements, transportability, maintainability and ease of development must be also considered.

The direct requirements for the HiLISP compiler are (1) runtime efficiency and (2) Common Lisp conformity. In other words, the target of HiLISP compiler is to realize rich facilities of Common Lisp, such as generic functions, without degrading performance. The Japanese language facility, which is implemented as built-in functions, and support environments, which are realized as utilities such as the editor and debugger, have little relation to the compiler.

There is a trade-off between high performance and other targets, such as memory efficiency or reliability. We decided that main process should be as fast as possible, and that other conflicting targets should be selected by options. For example, if a program contains function closures or multiple values, the program piece, which does not include such constructs, should escape degradation of performance. And if the high speed option is the top

priority, then **runtime** performance overrides compile time or memory efficiency.

The HiLISP system consists of an interpreter, I/O, built-in functions, a compiler, and utilities such as editor, and debugger. The interpreter executes a source program (S-expression), using its built-in functions. The HiLISP compiler accepts an S-expression and generates object code of machine instruction sequences. While compiling, it generates Lcode (Lisp intermediate code), which is a pseudo Lisp machine language, and LAP (Lisp Assembly Program), which is an intermediate language of assembler level.

The Lcode, which was created for the HiLISP compiler, is a machine code for a pseudo Lisp machine consisting of stacks, heaps and general registers. The operations are executed between registers and/or memory (heap and stack). The arguments are passed on a stack and the result is returned in a register.

Table 4.1 shows a summary of L-code, which is classified into function interfaces, variable accesses, stack operations, list operations, memory allocations, data accesses, branches, data definitions, utilities, and arithmetic operations that are excluded from the table. Most of the L-codes correspond to the primitives of Lisp.

By adapting Lcode, it becomes easier to transport compiler to other machines, and there is no need to worry about implementation details such as bit positions of tags, specific address of system constants, and register numbers, so on.

4.3 Compiling Optimization Methods

In order to clarify the problem spots in compiler optimization, Lisp programs were analyzed. In Lisp programs the ratio of functions calls (subroutine calls) to total runtime is generally thought to be higher than that in Fortran programs, and in the analysis we recognized it is not rare for the function call part to occupy more than half of the total execution time. Therefore the first goal was to speed up function calls. Secondly, in Lisp the frequency of built-in function calls is higher than in other languages (such as Fortran or Pascal), and lots of built-in functions are generic functions, which

Table.4.1 Summary of typical Lcode

#	Classification	Lcode	Remarks
1	Function interfaces	¥ ENTRY ¥ PREPARE ¥ CALL ¥ RETURN ¥ EVAL	function entry frame creation function call function call eval call
2	variable accesses	¥ VALUE ¥ SETVALUE ¥ INTERN ¥ BIND ¥ UNBIND	value reference value setting interning binding unbinding
3	stack operations	¥ PUSH ¥ POP ¥ ARGREF ¥ ARGSET	push pop argument reference argument setting
4	list operations	¥ CAR ¥ CDR ¥ CARSET ¥ CDRSET	car reference cdr reference car setting cdr setting
5	memory allocations	¥ CONS ¥ LIST	cons list
6	data accesses	¥ GETSYM ¥ GETSTR ¥ GETFIX	set symbol in register set string in register set fixnum in register
7	branches	¥ IFxxx ¥ GOTO	xxx is a data type, t, nil unconditional branch
8	data definitions	¥ END ¥ CONST ¥ SYMBOL	end of function constant definition symbol definition
9	utilities	¥ KEY ¥ GET ¥ TYPERROR	keyword param. match property list retrieval type error process

are common in Common Lisp. For generic functions, the goal was to reduce the runtime check overhead. Lastly, to run efficiently in main frame computers, it is necessary to utilize the pipeline capabilities, which can be achieved by local optimizations.

So the goals of the HiLISP compiler optimizations can summarized by three items:

(i) Function call optimizations

(ii) Type check optimizations

(iii) Local optimizations

138

In following sections, optimization methods for each goal are described.

(i) Function call optimizations

Two approaches are possible to attain function call optimizations; one is (a) reduction of calling time, the other is (b) reduction of number of calls.

In order to reduce function call time, the preparation time of the stack frame(for function call) and unframe process time (for function return) must be shortened as much as possible. We designed the function call instruction sequence and its machine cycle to be as short as possible, within the limits of the interface with the interpreter. We also partitioned the calling sequence into several short patterns depending on the callee's conditions, such as the self call, machine code call, and/or fixed number parameters. Therefore, the Lcode instruction ¥ call has several variations.

For reducing the number of calls , we applied the tail recursion removal method which is common in many Lisp compilers, enforced the inline expansion of built-in functions, and developed an automatic expansion method for self-inline functions and user function calls.

Here, self-recursion is a recursive call which calls itself directly, and tail recursion is a kind of self-recursion☆. Function expansion is theoretically similar to unfolding method formalized by Burstall and Darlington [4] for a functional language. There are some processors which execute expansions according to a user's instructions. There are problems for automatic function expansion described below, and few automatic expansion systems exist for practical programs. We designed our automatic function expansion method primarily for self-recursion, because Lisp programs have many self-recursions, because a definition body itself is easy to analyze, and because there is no problem of changing definitions.

-------- (note) -----------------------
☆) Tail recursion may call other functions, therefore tail recursion which calls itself directly is called, strictly speaking, tail self-recursion.

When performing expansion, the correctness of the **program** transformation and the possibility of degrading of performance are problems. The former problem includes the difficulties of (a) name conflicts after the expansion, (b) use of functions with side effect, such as nconc, (c) assignments to global variables; and the latter problem includes the difficulties of (d) increase in memory requirements, (e) increase in number of calls, and (f) trade-off with tail recursion removal.

The problem (e) is that if an actual parameter is a user function call or a "complex"☆ built-in function call and if the corresponding formal parameter appears more than once in the program, then the number of function calls will increase after the expansion. This problem is solved by using temporary variables. The problem (f) is deciding whether tail recursion removal is better than recursion expansion. We have judged that tail recursion removal is better from the point of view of memory efficiency.

From these considerations, the principles of self-recursion expansion are as follows. (The semantics of the transformation will be described later.)

(1)   Tail recursion shall not be expanded.

(2)   For the nested self-recursions, only the outer call shall be expanded.

(3)   The expansion shall be done only once for each call.

(4)   The expansion shall be done only for recursive calls in the function definition.

(5)   If there is a side effect ,such as an assignment of global variable, the expansion shall be refrained.

(6)   If the expanding part includes a user function call or a "complex" built-in function call, then a temporary variable shall be provided to hold function value.

-------- (note) ----------------------
☆) A "complex" built-in function call is one which is large enough that it cannot be expanded.

The figure 4.1 shows the detailed flow of self-recursion expansion based on these principles. First, a decision to expand or not is made by checking expandability (the existence of a self-recursion which is not tail recursion), correctness of the transformation (the existence of a side effect), and efficiency (program size). Next, each self-recursive call is expanded, if possible. At the expansion, local variable names are changed and temporary variables are used if they are necessary.

Figure 4.2 shows an example of self-recursive expansion, in which temporary variable w is used for each call of the built-in function *copy-tree* since it appears in the first argument of *l-tarai*. In many cases temporary variables are used. If a function call includes a function with side-effects, such as nconc, the temporary variable can be used to assemble multiple occurrences of function calls to prevent side-effects (Fig. 4.3).

Functions of Common Lisp are evaluated in applicative order and the parameters are passed by value, whereas functions of pure functional languages are evaluated in normal order and the parameters are passed by name. It is known that computation class of normal order is wider than that of applicative order [20]. Self-recursive expansion expands the function call part, which becomes normal-order evaluation and call by name. If the call part includes a function with a side effect, then the behavior of side effects may be changed by the change of evaluation order and parameter passing method. There is no need to check side effects in pure functional languages, which have no no side effect. In functional languages there is a transformation from normal order to applicative order to gain efficiency, and in such transformations it is necessary to check if the computation gets the same results or not. For the self-recursion expansion there is no problem like this, since the transformation is reverse, i.e. from applicative order to normal order. But in certain programs, the behavior may change after the transformation. For example a nonhalting program may halt after the expansion (Fig. 4.4). In this case use of temporary variable can avoid the problem, because if temporary variables are used to calculated all

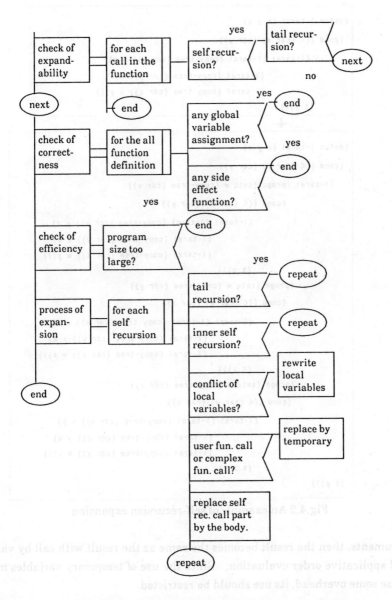

Fig.4.1. An algorithm of self recursive expansion

arguments, then the result becomes the same as the result with call by value and applicative order evaluation. use of temporary variables may cause some overhead. its use should be restricted

```
(defun 1-tarai (x y z)
  (cond ((< (car x) (car y))
         (1-tarai (1-tarai (copy-tree (cdr x)) y z)
                  (1-tarai (copy-tree (cdr y)) z x)
                  (1-tarai (copy-tree (cdr z)) x y)))
        (t y)))
```

↓

```
(defun 1-tarai (x y z)
  (cond ((< (car x) (car y))
         (1-tarai (progn (setq w (copy-tree (cdr x)))
                    (cond ((< (car w) (car y))
                           (1-tarai (1-tarai (copy-tree (cdr w)) y z)
                                    (1-tarai (copy-tree (cdr y)) z w)
                                    (1-tarai (copy-tree (cdr z)) w y)))
                          (t y)))
                  (progn (setq w (copy-tree (cdr y)))
                    (cond ((< (car w) (car z))
                           (1-tarai (1-tarai (copy-tree (cdr w)) z x)
                                    (1-tarai (copy-tree (cdr y)) x w)
                                    (1-tarai (copy-tree (cdr z)) w z)))
                          (t z)))
                  (progn (setq w (copy-tree (cdr z)))
                    (cond ((< (car w) (car x))
                           (1-tarai (1-tarai (copy-tree (cdr w)) x y)
                                    (1-tarai (copy-tree (cdr z)) y w)
                                    (1-tarai (copy-tree (cdr y)) w x)))
                          (t x)))))
        (t y)))
```

Fig.4.2 An example of self-recursion expansion

arguments, then the result becomes the same as the result with call by value
and applicative order evaluation. Since the use of temporary variables may
cause some overhead, its use should be restricted.

```
      (defun foo (x y)
       (if (> (length y) 5) y
               (list (foo x (nconc x y)))))))   ·····(a)
      (defun foo (x y)
       (if (> (length y) 5) y
               (list (if (> (length (nconc x y)) 5)(nconc x y)
                    (list (foo x (nconc x y (nconc x y)))))))))
                                                ····· (b)
     (defun foo (x y)
      (if (> (length y) 5) y
              (list (let ((w (nconc x y)))
                       (if (> (length w) 5) w
                          (list (foo x w)))))))··(c)
     (foo '(1 2 3) '(4 5 6))
     =>((1 2 3 4 5 6))                          ·····(a),(c)
     =>((1 2 3 4 5 6 4 5 6 ·····))              ·····(b)
```

Fig. 4.3   An example of the expansion of a self-recursive function with a side effect.

```
     (defun baa (x y)
      (if (= x 0) 1 (1+ (baa (1- x)(baa (- x y)y)))))
```

Fig. 4.4 An example of a function which does not halt.

(ii) Type check optimization

In order to optimize runtime type checking in Lisp, there are two methods; one is (a) the reduction of type check time at runtime, and the other is (b) the compile-time type check.

The reduction of type check time at runtime is achieved by a preference for more frequent tag check earlier and by reorder of instruction sequence to

minimize the branch time after checking. The latter was implemented as a part of local optimizations.

The compile time type check for reduction of run time type check is realized by identifying the types of data or operations with type checking and type inference, based on the users declaration information and other available informations.

The rules of type check and type inference at compile time are as follows:

(a) Check types of variables from the type declarations.

(b) Check types of functions which have unique types.

(c) Infer types of arguments which correspond to parameters with unique types..

(d) Infer types of generic functions for which the types of operations or the types of result are derived by the types of arguments.

(e) Infer types from combinations of the above rules.

If type is established at the beginning, as in (a), (b), it is called a type check, and in all other cases it is called a type inference. Type inference by combination (e) operates in general from inside to outside, using (a), (b) and (d) and if the type is unknown, then (c) is used to infer from outside to inside. Type specification by Common Lisp's "*the*" is a variation of (b).

Figure 4.5 shows a simple example of type check and type inference. Reverse is a generic function which reverses an array, string, or list, and the type of operation and type of result are determined by its argument. In the example, *sort* is another generic function whose type is determined by the type of its first argument. First, a type check of the argument of *sort* is performed. Then the result type of *sort*, that is, the argument type of *reverse*, is inferred. Finally, the operation type and result type of *reverse* is inferred to be a list.

As a result of type checks and type inferences, ranges of operation types are restricted, and some built-in functions, which are normally called as generic functions, can be expanded inline.

Types in Common Lisp are basically dynamic types which are attached to objects, plus some auxiliary type informations are supplied by the user.

Therefore, types are not always as completely decidable as they **are in** strongly-typed languages, like Pascal or Ada. Nevertheless, reducing the runtime type checking is one of the most important speedup methods of optimizing compilers for Common Lisp, in which generic functions are used frequently.

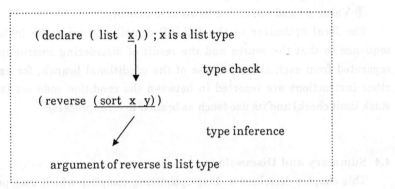

Fig.4.5 An example of type check and type inference

(iii) Local optimization

The local optimization of HiLISP is classified into the optimization in Lcode level (Local-opt1) and the optimization in LAP level (Local-opt2).

Local-opt1 optimizes Lcode locally in a machine-independent way. The main optimizations are as follows:

(a)   Reduction of unnecessary codes.

(b)   Optimization of branch codes.

(c)   Reduction of stack limit checks.

Stack limit code is reduced by combining multiple stack limit checks. Branch optimization is done by reversing the test condition if the then part is unconditional branch and by unifying multiple branches, etc.

Local-opt2 optimizes LAP code locally in a machine-dependent way. The main optimizations are as follows:

(a)   Reduction of unnecessary instructions.

(b)   Reordering of instruction sequences.

Mainframe computers have a powerful pipeline control mechanism which executes most operations effectively in one machine cycle. But if the pipeline is disordered, then the execution time becomes slower than one cycle. The typical cause of disordering are as follows:

① Condition code set and its use (conditional branch).

② Index register/base register set and their use.

③ Value set and use in one location in memory.

The local optimizer in the HiLISP compiler reorder the instruction sequence so that the source and the result of disordering instructions are separated from each other. In case of the conditional branch, for example, other instructions are inserted in between the condition code set (such as stack limit check) and its use (such as branch to error process).

4.4 Summary and Discussions

This chapter described a Lisp optimizing compiler which uses program transformations. The Lisp dialect is Common Lisp. Optimizations are performed for function calls, type checkings, and local optimizations. The algorithm of self inline expansion for function call optimization has been developed as one of the program transformations, and its detail is described. The most popular inline expansion is that of built-in functions, which is effective and frequently used in many Lisp optimizing compilers. Inline expansion of user functions is usually performed at the users' option; few optimizing compiler performs automatic expansion. There are no reports of self inline expansion in Lisp optimizing compilers. Self inline expansion is theoretically clarified by fixed point recursion theory [20], but there is no practical compiler which implements the method. The unfold method advocated by Burstall, Darlington is close in concept with expansion. The differences of their method with self inline expansion are that Burstall and Darlington applied their method to a pure functional language, that their system is not an automatic one, and that they applied unfolding other function calls, not self-recursions.

5. IMPLEMENTATION AND EVALUATION

5.1 Implementation and Evaluation of Loop Splitting

The automatic loop splitting method described in chapter 2 has been implemented in HITAC M200H and M280H as the part of its extended vectorization features. Though its complete evaluation will be a subject for future study, the applicability of the algorithm is analyzed for 45 scientific benchmark programs.

In the 45 benchmark programs, there are 43 loops which are the object of loop splitting, and among them 23 loops contain promoted variables. This indicates that the frequency of promoted variables is relatively high. Among the 43 loops only 2 loops have 2 split points, and all others have only one split point, and this indicates that the overhead of multiple splits is not serious. The average vectorization ratio of the split DO loops is 47%.

The performance gain by loop splitting cannot be measured at this point, since the loop splitting is implemented with other extensions. This evaluation must be done in the future.

5.2 Implementation and Evaluation of Extension to Data Dependency Analysis

The part of the data dependency analysis method described in chapter 3 has been implemented in the compiler for M280H IAP, and most of it is implemented in the vector compiler for the S-810.

In M280H IAP compiler, loop splitting, loop expansions, vectorization of IF statements are implemented, where the vectorization of nested IF statements is restricted for efficiency and the data flow within an IF statement is based on depth-first traversing.

In the S-810 vector compiler, not only loop splitting, loop expansions, and vectorization of IF statements, but also statement exchange and vector object optimization are implemented. For the vectorization of IF statements, there is no restriction on the nested IF statements, and the data flow within IF statement is based on breadth-first traversal described in chapter 3.

Optimization methods for vector objects are described in following paragraphs.

Object optimization techniques for vector compilers are vector text optimizations, vector register assignments, vector memory management, and other machine-dependent optimizations.

Vector text optimization is a common technique for the IAP and the S-810 vector processor, and it is similar to scalar text optimization. Some of the vector text optimization techniques are common expression elimination, invariant expression move-out, and dead code elimination. Among them the first two are most effective for vector processors.

Vector register assignment is the one of the important tasks for the S-810 type vector processor. Vector memory management is the important task for IAP type vector processors. The main target of vector memory management is the efficient use of the temporary vectors in memory.

Examples of machine dependent optimization for the S-810 are:

(1) Use of the VMA (Vector Multiply with scalar and Add) instruction instead of the VM (Vector Multiply) with scalar and the VA (Vector Add) instructions.

(2) Parallel execution of vector instructions with their preparing instructions (Fig. 5.1). Here the TestVp instruction, which will wait the end of vector instructions, is moved out from the outer DO loop.

(3) Compression of vector arguments for intrinsic functions under IF statements (Fig. 5.2). The argument is composed of those elements, each of which corresponds to the true case of IF-expression.

Among these optimization techniques, the vector register assignment is the most important and most difficult one. Little has been reported on vector register assignment. The strategy should be different from scalar register assignment, since vector processors like the S-810 execute multiple vector instructions in parallel and the access to the same vector register by different instructions may hinder their parallel execution. The vector instruction specification also imposes some restrictions on the vector register assignment for each instruction. Thus we employ tabulated LRU (Least Recently Used) method to assign vector registers, in place of simple Round-Robin.

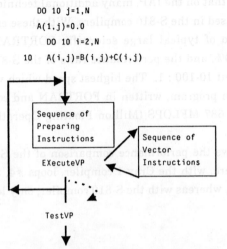

```
            DO 10 j=1,N
            A(1,j)=0.0
            DO 10 i=2,N
        10  A(i,j)=B(i,j)+C(i,j)
```

Fig. 5.1 scalar/vector parallel execution

```
            DO 10 i=1,N
            IF(A(i).NE.0) THEN
              B(i)=SQRT(A(i))
            ENDIF
        10 CONTINUE
```

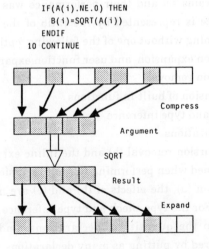

Fig. 5.2 A compression of built-in function argument

Though the basic algorithm of the data dependency analysis on the S-810 is the same as that on the IAP, many additional techniques of enhancing vectorization are used in the S-810 compilers. With these enhancements, the vectorization ratio of typical large scientific FORTRAN programs has increased about 30%, and the performance ratio of the S-810 vector mode to scalar mode is about 10-100 : 1. The highest speed which was attained for a thermal conduction program, written in FORTRAN and compiled by the S-810 compiler, was 687 MFLOPS (Million Floating Operations Per Second) 11).

Table 5.1 shows the performance comparison of the S-810 with that of the Cray-1 12). Here, with the Cray-1 compiler, loops #4, 5, 6, 8, 11, 13, 14 are unvectorizable, whereas with the S-810 compiler, only loops #5 and 6 are unvectorizable.

5.3 Implementation and Evaluation of Lisp Compiling Optimization

In order to evaluate the performance of optimizing algorithms of HiLISP compiler described in chapter 4, 12 benchmark programs were selected from the Lisp contest programs 23) and their performance was measured (Table 5.2). The performance is represented by the ratio of the timing with full optimization to the timing without one of the following optimizations:

(a)   Self-recursion expansion and user function expansion
(b)   Tail recursion removal
(c)   Inline expansion of built-in functions
(d)   Type check and type inference
(e)   Local optimizations

Since the tail recursion removal (b) and the inline expansion of built-in functions (c) are assumed when performing the self-recursion expansion and user function expansion (a), the effects of (b) and (c) are measured without the optimization (a). For the type check and type inference optimization, the effects may depend on the quantity of declarations, and the benchmark programs were measured by putting as many declarations as the same level with the benchmark programs written in a older Lisp (MacLisp dialect).

Table 5.1 Livermore Loops on the CRAY-1 and the S-810 [Kara84]

#	DO LOOP	Cray CRAY-1 MFLOPS	HITAC S-810/20 MFLOPS	Ratio H/C	Vectorizing* Cray	Vectorizing* S810
1	Hydro excerpt	69.4	246.8	3.56	Yes	Yes
2	MLR. Inner product	40.3	255.3	6.33	Yes	Yes
3	Inner product	27.5	213.3	7.76	Yes	Yes
4	Banded linear eq.	3.6	60.6	16.83	No	Yes
5	Tri-diag. elim. (lower)	7.2	4.9	0.68	No	No
6	Tri-diag. elim. (upper)	6.7	4.2	0.63	No	No
7	Eq. of state excerpt	78.0	254.6	3.26	Yes	Yes
8	P. D. E. integration	13.3	77.5	5.83	No	Yes
9	Integer predictor	56.7	226.7	4.00	Yes	Yes
10	Difference predictor	29.2	57.9	1.98	Yes	Yes
11	First summation	2.7	9.8	3.63	No	Yes
12	First difference	23.0	106.4	4.63	Yes	Yes
13	2-D particle pusher	3.6	4.2	1.17	No	Yes
14	1-D particle pusher	6.1	7.8	1.28	No	Yes
	Average	26.2	109.3	4.17		
	Data length(bits)	64	64			
	observation Date	6/81	10/83			
	Computer Center	Cray Inc	UnivTokyo			

NOTE:Average = Total sum of each MFLOPS / Number of LOOPs (14).
Ratio = MFLOPS value on S-810 model20 / MFLOPS value on CRAY-1.
*Vectorizing result is commented by the autor.

The effect of the self-recursion expansion and user function expansion sped the program by 8%, the tail recursion removal by 9%, the inline expansion of built-in functions by 157%, the type check and type inference by 32%, and the local optimizations by 6%, in geometric means in 12 benchmark programs.

The most effective optimization is the inline expansion of built-in functions, as was expected. The next most effective one is the type checking and type inference, because it not only removes type check codes but also gives compound effects by producing inline expansions and by avoiding unnecessary saves to the stack (which were required for GC).

The effect of the self-recursion expansion and user function expansion is almost the same as the tail recursion removal, and it indicates that the function calls are frequent in Lisp.

The effect of local optimization fell short of expectation. This is because instruction sequences expanded from Lcode have already been arranged so that the pipeline is active as much as possible.

Overheads of optimizations are increase of object size, increase of compiler size , and increase of compile time. In the HiLISP compiler the increase of object size and the increase of compiler size are about 20% each,but the increase of compile time is about 3 times, which can be improved by a minor modification of optimizer.

As for the absolute performance of the HiLISP compiler object, it is reported that HiLISP is faster than the fastest Lisp processor of the Lisp contest on a same machine [34].

Tbl.5.2 Performance of HiLISP Compiler for Benchmarks of the Lisp Contest

Bench-mark	① all optimization	② w/o self rec. & user func. exp.	③ w/o tail rec. remov. +②	④ w/o builtin func. exp. +②	⑤ w/o type inf.& check	⑥ w/o local optimization	ratio				
							$\frac{②}{①}$	$\frac{③}{②}$	$\frac{④}{②}$	$\frac{⑤}{①}$	$\frac{⑥}{①}$
tarai-5	129 ms	213 ms	312 ms	932 ms	360 ms	151 ms	1.65	1.46	4.38	2.79	1.17
list-tarai	23.5	25.9	30.1	64.9	28.7	24.6	1.10	1.16	2.51	1.22	1.05
s-tarai	137	140	143	199	176	138	1.02	1.02	1.42	1.28	1.01
flo-tarai	11.7	13.8	17.9	67.4	22.0	11.7	1.18	1.30	4.88	1.88	1.00
Sort	3.32	3.24	3.28	13.73	4.77	3.71	0.98	1.01	4.24	1.44	1.12
Seq-100	3.53	3.50	3.59	4.90	3.67	3.58	0.99	1.11	1.40	1.04	1.01
BITA-6	0.86	0.85	0.85	3.79	0.92	0.92	0.99	1.00	4.46	1.07	1.07
Sort-100	0.12	0.12	0.12	0.12	0.12	0.12	1.00	1.00	1.00	1.00	1.00
TPU-6	113.4	114.8	119.3	218.8	124.7	118.2	1.01	1.04	1.91	1.10	1.04
Prolog-sort	18.7	22.9	23.0	58.7	26.6	19.6	1.22	1.00	2.56	1.42	1.05
Diff-5	19.7	19.5	20.1	48.8	22.7	21.5	0.99	1.03	2.50	1.15	1.09
Boyer	751	770	847	2624	873	860	1.03	1.10	3.41	1.16	1.15
geometric mean	-	-	-	-	-	-	1.08	1.09	2.57	1.32	1.06

M680H

Though in Common Lisp there are some factors, such as intensification of generic functions, which may render slow execution time, a fast language processor can be made on a stock hardware, and almost the same speed can be attained in Lisp compared with in procedural language such as Pascal or C (☆), if the processor is well constructed.

The proposed optimizing methods are useful for Lisp compilers, especially for Common Lisp compilers, and they will be used by many Lisp compilers in future.

The HiLISP compiler which was designed and implemented this time is a subset which does not includes bignum and multiple values. The adaption of these features may degrade the performance, but it is estimated that the degradation is not no large. Based on the prototype of the HiLISP system, the product system with almost the full set is been developed and its performance will be measured.

5.4 Summary and Discussions

The M200H, M280H IAP compiler is the first compiler to implement partial vectorization by loop splitting. Loop splitting was applied for 45 scientific programs, and 43 DO loops were split. It was found that in many cases (23/43) there were promoted variables, and that multiple fragmentations are rare (2/43). The effect of loop splitting is not remarkable in the IAP where the performance ratio of vector to scalar is not high. The loop split algorithm was transferred to the vector compiler for the S-810, where the performance ratio of vector to scalar is high and it is important to

-------- (note) ----------------------

☆Performance comparison of Lisp with Pascal -- Table 5.3 shows performance comparison of Lisp with Pascal for six benchmark programs. In geometric mean, the ratio of performance is almost the same. Lisp is faster in *tak*, which has a great deal of self-recursion and in which tail-recursion removal and self-recursion expansion are effective. As the data for *Qsort* and *Nqueen* indicate, in general Lisp is faster in list versions and Pascal is faster in array version.

Table 5.3 Performance comparison of Lisp with Pascal

#	Benchmark	HiLISP	Pascal8000	ratio (P/L)
1	Tak	41. *ms*	69. *ms*	1.68
2	Flo-tarai-4	22.	20.	0.91
3	Qsort-100 (list version)	37.	66.	1.8
4	Bubble-50 (array version)	5.3	2.6	0.49
5	Nqueen-8 (list version)	95.	304.	3.2
6	Nqueen-8 (array version)	53.	25.	0.47
	Geometric Mean	–	–	1.15

M680H

increase vectorization ratio as much as possible to increase total performance.

The algorithms and techniques for the extension to the data dependency analysis are implemented in the S-810 vector compiler. The M280H IAP compiler is the first compiler which automatically vectorizes conditional statements. The S-810 vector compiler was shipped in October, 1983 as the first vector compiler for a supercomputer in Japan. The vectorization ratio it attained is higher than that of the vector compiler for the Cray-1, which was the first vector supercomputer in the world. For example, in the Livermore 14 loops, 12 loops can be vectorized in the S-810 compiler, whereas only 7 loops can be vectorized in the Cray-1 compiler. This is because of the extensions of vectorization based on the basic data dependency algorithm, with the enhancements by program transformations such as partial vectorization, loop expansion and statement exchanges.

The optimization algorithms of Lisp compiler are implemented in the HiLISP compiler for Common Lisp. Based on the prototype of HiLISP system, the product system (VOS3 Lisp) has been developed and it is the first Common Lisp system developed by computer manufacturer in Japan. The first Common Lisp system in Japan was KCL (Kyoto Common Lisp) . The compiler of KCL is a translator to C and it does not handle declarations (except declaration of special variables). An optimization is limited to inline expansion of built-in functions [8]. The first Common Lisp system in the world was the experimental S-1 system [3], and Spice Lisp [40] was the first practical system. The Spice Lisp was developed as a portable kit and it was distributed mostly in America as a basis of Common Lisp system. Little is reported about the compiler, but its intermediate language [40] is close to Lcode. The S-1 Common Lisp compiler performs several source level program transformations, for example it derives short circuit evaluation codes by introducing lambda expressions. It also optimizes code by constant folding and by removal of useless code, but has no peephole optimization. The tail recursion removal is naturally included [3].

6. CONCLUSION

The purpose of the study is to add the program transformation methods into the repertoire of optimizing compilers. Precisely speaking, it asserts that the vectorization is in fact a program transformation, that the vectorization can be expanded by introducing program transformations, such as partial vectorization and loop expansions, etc., and that an optimizing compiler for Common Lisp can also be enhanced by introducing program transformations, such as self-inline expansion.

In other words, vectorization, which is a practical concern for compiler, can be addressed by program transformation; and program transformation methods which had a theoretical role in handling transformation in pure functional languages, can also be used for practical compiling optimizations. Meanwhile, the algorithms such as the partial vectorization algorithm and the breadth-first data flow analysis have been developed.

7. ACKNOWLEDGEMENTS

The author would like to thank Jim Delahunt for his valuable comments during the preparation of this manuscript.

REFERENCES

1. Aho, A. V., Ullman, J. D., "Principles of Compiler Design", Addison-Wesley, 604, (1977).

2. Allen, J. R., "Anatomy of Lisp", McGraw-Hill, (1978).

3. Brooks, R. A., Gabriel, R. P., Steele, G. L. Jr., "An Optimizing Compiler for Lexically Scoped LISP", Proc. of the 1982 ACM Compiler Construction Conf., 261-274, (1982).

4. Burstall, R. M., Darlington, J., "A Transformation System for Developing Recursive Programs", J. ACM, 24, 1, 44-67, (Jan. 1977).

5. Chikayama, T., "Implementation of the UtiLisp System", Trans. of IPSJ, 24, 3, 599-604 (in Japanese), (1983).

6. Darlington, J., "Program Transformation", Functional Programming and its Applications, Ed. by J. Darlington, et. al, Cambridge Univ. Press, (1982).

7. Gries, D., "Compiler Construction for Digital Computers", John Wiley & Sons Inc., 493, (1971).

8. Hagiya, M., Yuasa, T., "Implementation of Kyoto Common Lisp", 1st Conf. Proc. of Japan Society for Software Science and Technology, 65-68 (in Japanese), (1984).

9. Horikoshi, H., Umetani, Y., "Integrated Vector Arithmetic Facility for General purpose Computer", Trans. of IPSJ, 24, . 2, 191-199 (in Japanese), (Mar. 1983).

10. Horikoshi, H., Umetani, Y., "Conditional Vector Arithmetic Facility for General Purpose Computer", Trans. of IPSJ, 24, 4, 531-541 (in Japanese), (Jul. 1983).

11. Karaki, Y., "Effective Use of the Super-computer", Center News, Computer Centre, University of Tokyo, 15, 9-10, 39-62 (in Japanese), (1983).

12. Karaki, Y, "Characteristics of the S-810 Super Computer", Super Computer Workshop Report 3, Computer Center, Institute for Molecular Science, 24-41 (in Japanese), (Aug. 1984).

13. Knuth, D. E., "An Empirical Study of FORTRAN Programs", Software - Practice and Experience, 1, 2, 105-133, (1971).

158

14. Kuck, D. J., "Parallel Processing of Ordinary Programs", Advances in Computer, Academic Press, 15, 119-179, (1976).

15. Kuck, D., Kuhn, R., Padua, D., Leasure, B., Wolf, M., "Dependence Graphs and Compiler Optimizations", Proc. of the 8th ACM Symp. on Princ. of Programming Languages, (1981).

16. Kozdrowicki, E, W., Theis, D. J., "Second Generation of Vector Super Computers", IEEE Computer, 13, 11, . 71-83, (Nov. 1980).

17. Lamport, L., "Parallel Execution of DO Loops", Comm. ACM, 17, 2, 83-92, (1974).

18. Loveman, D. B., "Program Improvement by Source-to-Source Transformation", J. ACM, 20, 1, 121-145, (1977).

19. Lowry, E., Medlock, C. W., "Object Code Optimization", Comm. ACM, 12, 1, 13-22, (1969).

20. Manna, Z., "Mathematical Theory of Computation", McGraw-Hill, 448, (1974).

21. Nakata, I., "Compiler", Sangyou Tosho, 278 (in Japanese), (1981).

22. JEIDA (Japan Electronic Industry Development Association), Ed., "The Report of the Surveys on Micro Computers [II] - Common Lisp - ", 61-A-235 [II], 155 (in Japanese), (1986).

23. Okuno, H., "The Proposal of the benchmarks for the third Lisp Contest and the first Prolog Contest", Preprints of WGSYM, 28-4, IPSJ (in Japanese), (1984).

24. Okuno, H., "The Report of the Third Lisp Contest and the First Prolog Contest", Preprints of WGSYM, IPSJ, 85, 30, (1985).

25. Padua, D. A., Kuck, D. J., Lawrie, D. H., "High-Speed Multi-processors and Compilation Techniques", IEEE Trans. on Computer, C-29, 763-776, (Sept. 1980).

26. Partisch, H., Steinburger, R., "Program Transformation Systems", ACM Computing Surveys, 15, 3, (1983).

27. Sato, T., Tamaki, H., "Program transformation in Prolog", Proc. of the Logic Programming Conf. 83 (in Japanese), (1983).

28. Sato, T., Tamaki, H., "Transformational Logic Program Syntheses", Proc. of the International Conf. of Fifth Generation Computer Systems, 195-201, (1984).

29. Sites, R. L., "An Analysis of the CRAY-1 Computer", Proc. of the 5th Annual Symp. on Computer Architecture, 101-106, (1978).

30. Steele, G. L. Jr., "Common Lisp : the Language", Digital Press, 645 (1984).

31. Takanuki, R., Umetani, Y., Nakata, I., "Some Compiling Algorithms for Array Processor", Proc. of 3rd USA Japan Computer Conf., 273-279, (1978).

32. Takanuki, R., Umetani, Y., "Optimizing FORTRAN77", Hitachi Review, 30, 5, 241-246, (1981).

33. Takada, A., Yasumura, M., Aoshima, T., "New scheme of high speed code generation for HiLISP compiler", 3rd Conf. Proc. of Japan Society for Software Science and Technology (in Japanese), 97-100 (1986).

34. Takeichi, N., Yasumura, M., Yuura, K., Morita, K., "High Performance List Processor System", The Hitachi Hyoron, 69, 3, 13-16 (in Japanese), (Mar. 1987).

35. Umetani, Y., Kawabe, S., Horikoshi, H., Odaka, T.,, "An Analysis on Applicability of the Vector Operations to Scientific Programs and the Determination of an Effective Instruction Repertoire", Proc. of 3rd USA Japan Computer Conf., 331-335, (1978).

36. Umetani, Y., Takanuki, T., Horikoshi, H., "Vector Machines and Vectorizing Methods in Vector Compilers", The technical report of WG, IECE (Inst. Electronics and Comm. Eng.), EC 80-15, 49-56 (in Japanese), (Jun. 1980).

37. Umetani, Y., Takanuki, T., Yasumura, M., "Automatic Vectorization Techniques for Scientific Programs", Proc. of Information Processing, 23, 1, 29-40 (in Japanese), (Jan. 1982).

38. Umetani, Y., Horikoshi, H., "Automatic Vectorizing Compiler for Integrated Vector Arithmetic Facility", Trans. of Information Processing, 24, 2, 238-248 (in Japanese), (Mar. 1983).

39. Umetani, Y., Yasumura, M., "A Vectorization Algorithm for Control Statements", J. of Information Processing, 7, 3, 170-174, (1984).

40. Wholey, S., Fahlman, S. E., "The Design of an Instruction Set for Common Lisp", Conf. Record of the 1984 ACM Symp. on Lisp and Functional Programming, 150-158, (1984).

160

41.   Yasumura, M., Matsunaga, T., Tanaka, Y., Umetani, Y., "A Method of Control Flow Analysis for Vector Compilers", Proc. 23rd Annual Convention of IPSJ, 211-212 (in Japanese), (Oct. 1981).

42.   Yasumura, M., Umetani, Y., Horikoshi, H., "Partial Vectorization Method for Automatic Vector Compilers", Trans. of Information Processing (in Japanese), 24, 1, (Jan. 1983).

43.   Yasumura, M., Tanaka, Y., Kanada, Y., Aoyama, A., "Compiling Algorithms and Techniques for the S-810 Vector Processor", IEEE Proc. of International Conf. of Parallel Processing 84, 285-290, (1984).

44.   Yasumura, M., "Vectorization and Program transformation", The Summer Symp. on Program composition, transformation and reusing, IPSJ, 89-98 (in Japanese), (July 1985).

45.   Yasumura, M., Takada, A., Yuura, K., "Program Transformation Techniques in Recursive Programs", Riken Symp. on Functional Programming, FP-87-03, 20-27 (in Japanese), (1987).

46.   Yasumura, M., Takada, A., Aoshima, T., "Design and Implementation of an Optimizing Compiler for Common Lisp", Trans. of Information Processing, 28, 11 (in Japanese), (Nov. 1987).

47.   Yuasa, T., Hagiya, M., "Implementation of Kyoto Common Lisp", Preprints of WGSYM, IPSJ, 34-1 (in Japanese), (1985).

48.   Yuura, K., Yasumura, M., "High Speed Methods for the HiLISP Interpreter", Preprints of WGSYM, IPSJ, 40-5 (in Japanese), (1987).

Part 4
Hardware Technology for Supercomputing

Quantum Flux Parametron and Neural Network Modelling

A Proposed Generalization of the Topology of the Connection Machine

Preliminary Study of the CPU Performance of the TITAN Compared with that of the Cray X-MP/1

Quantum Flux Parametron and Neural Network Modelling

E.Goto[*,#] and K.F.Loe[+,#]

*Dept of Information Science, University of Tokyo,
+DISCS, National University of Singapore
#Quantum Magneto Flux Logic Project, Research Development Corp. of Japan
#Information Science Lab., The Institute of Physical and Chemical Research

Abstract

Quantum Flux Parametron(QFP) is a Josephson junction device based on the logic and amplification principle of parametron. The device can be used for making a highly sensitive sensor for magnetic brain wave measurement as well as for high speed parallel pipeline computer design. QFP computer realizes a high pitch pipeline control with a very high speed clock of 10GHz without using the conventional pipeline registers due to the fact that QFP also functions as a latch(register). Cyclic Pipeline Computer is an architecture being designed taking advantage of the characteristics of QFP. The potential of using such a computer for more realistic simulation of the neurocomputing will be discussed.

Quantum Flux Parametron(QFP) is a Josephson junction Device which can be used as a kind of majority logic device to realize the computaional operations such as AND and OR operations[1,2]. Together with flux inverting transformer which serves as the negation logical operations, all kinds of logical circuits necessary for building a very high speed computer can be realized. The memory device is constructed using dc-SQUID, a Josephson junction device, to store a quantum flux as one bit of information and QFPs are used for controlling the READ and WRITE of the quantum flux[3]. Thus a highly integrated high speed computer designed in this way will operate in the cryogenic environment.

Figure 1 shows the basic circuit elements of a QFP, where ϕ_1 and ϕ_2 are the phase differences over two identical Josephson junctions, Φ_S is the input flux, Φ_E is the excitation clocking flux and Φ is the output flux. The potential energy of the system is given by,

164

$$U_0 = \frac{(\Phi - \Phi_S)^2}{2L} - \frac{I_m \Phi_0}{2\pi}(\cos\phi_1 + \cos\phi_2)$$

The above expression can be simplified if we let

$$E = 2\pi\frac{\Phi_E}{\Phi_o}, \quad S = 2\pi\frac{\Phi_S}{\Phi_o}, \quad \phi = 2\pi\frac{\Phi}{\Phi_o}, \quad \phi_1 = 2\pi\frac{\Phi_1}{\Phi_o}, \quad \phi_2 = 2\pi\frac{\Phi_2}{\Phi_o}$$

$$I_m = \frac{\Phi_o}{2\pi L_J}, \quad L = \frac{A}{2}L_J, \quad E_J = \frac{\Phi_o^2}{4\pi^2 L_J}, \quad \phi_1 = \phi + E, \quad \phi_2 = \phi - E$$

so that the potential can be written in terms of three dimensionless variables S, E and ϕ which correspond to the input, clocking and output signals respectively, i.e.,

$$U_0 = E_J[\frac{(\phi - S)^2}{A} - 2\cos E \cos\phi]$$

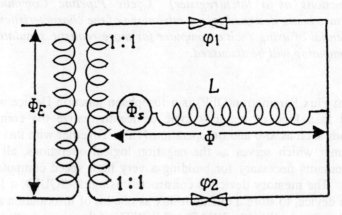

Fig.1 A schematic drawing of a QFP

Given an input signal s and prior to the application of excitation E, the above potential U_o looks like Fig. 2(a), with only an absolute minimum. When E is applied and rising to a critical value E_c the potential changes to Fig.2(b) with an absolute minimum and a turning point ϕ_t. When $E > E_c$ double-well potential emerges as shown in Fig.2(c). The maximum at ϕ_p is the potential barrier between the metastable minimum ϕ_m and the absolute minimum ϕ_a. The device is operated by a clock excitation signal of amplitude π connected to E. When the clock signal rises up to its full value of π the output signal reaches the steady state and the amplified output signal is given by ϕ_a. On the other hand if an inverse input signal $-s$ is applied then $-\phi_a$ is obtained as an inverse binary logic state, as shown in Fig.2(d).

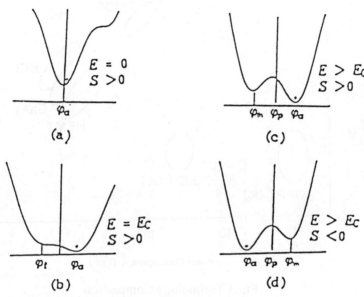

Fig.2 Potential states

Simulation on the logical operations of the device with three phase clock have shown the feasibility of QFP logic device. Experiment on some of these devices have also been done in the Hitachi Central Research Laboratory and confirmed the simulated results[3]. These experiments included operation of a three-stage circuit driving by three phase clock, inverter circuit and majority logic circuit. The power consumption of QFP was found to be much more lower than the existing known technology used for computer design as shown in Fig.3. Thus a highly integrated computer can be designed using the QFP without serious heat dissipating problem. Cyclic Pipeline Computer to be designed using the QFP technology will have QFP logic circuit of 10^4 placed on a card of 1 cm^2 in area and 100μm in thickness. Signal transfer between cards is realized by using coils which are placed in the surface of cards so that they form flux transformers when stack together. The Cyclic Pipeline Computer with a memory of 10^9bits and 40 processors would have the 3-D cubical structure. The processors occupy the volume of 1 cm cube surrounded by the memory so that the whole computer occupies a size of 5 cm cube.

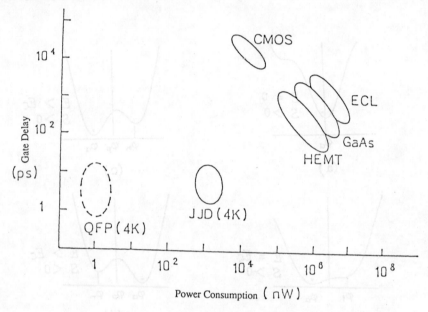

Fig.3 Technology Comparison

The Cyclic Pipeline Computer[4] to be built using the QFP technology is different from the conventional supercomputer in some essential aspects coming from the latching characteristics of the Josephson junction devices. Information manipulated by a Josephson junction device is a flux trapped in a loop, therefore a QFP not only serves as a logic device based on the polarities of the flux to represent binary information, it also functions as a latch. For this reason, QFP can also be used to build memory and memory control devices. Therefore there are two aspects which make the design of QFP supercomputer different from the conventional supercomputer. In the conventional supercomputer the speed for memory access does not match up with the CPU operation. Thus pipeline registers are required to realize pipeline operation resulting in additional delay time. In the conventional pipeline computers, in order to minimize the delays caused by the insertion of registers, a rather long sequence of basic logic gates are placed in between the pipeline registers.

In the case of the QFP supercomputer, the memory read and write control would also be designed using the QFP device, thus the processors and the memory can both be pipelined with the same pipeline pitch time. In addition QFP also functions as a latch(register), therefore no extra delays is incurred by adopting the high pitch and shallow pipeline logic in the architecture design. In fact the natural choice of the pipeline pitch time is the basic clocking of $\tau = 100ps$ used for the QFP majority logic operation. Therefore the cache memory or pipeline register does not physically exist as the additional components in the QFP type of computer systems. Cyclic Pipeline Computer(CPC) is a machine which was conceived taking advantage of the characteristics of QFP device[4]. The schematic diagram showing the pipeline of a processor and common main memory is shown in Fig.4, where τ is the pipeline pitch time. If the memory access and the advanced control of a processor take M_1 and M_2 units of pipeline pitch time τ to complete their operations respectively, then a total of $M=M_1+M_2$ processors can timeshare the memory access and instruction execution without memory access conflict. Thus CPC is actually equivalent to a multiprocessor system with M processors which share a common main memory system.

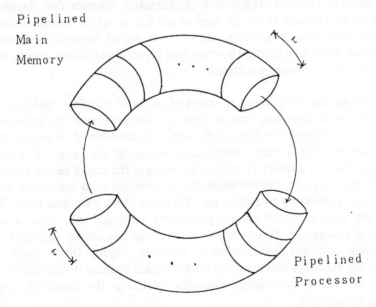

Pipelined
Main
Memory

Pipelined
Processor

Fig.4 A schematic diagram of cyclic pipeline operation

QFP could become a useful tool for research on the neural network. In the current research of brain science, SQUID circuit is used for detecting the extremely weak magnetic brain wave emitted by brain activities. Experiments done with QFP as a magnetic brain wave sensor have shown that the sensivity of QFP as a sensing device is at least 30% higher than the current SQUID sensor[5,6].

Among other applications, Cyclic Pipeline Computer to be built with QFP may bring up the simulation of neurocomputing to a more realistic level. It is known neurocomputing is inspired by the structure of human brain. Though there are different models of neural network being proposed, the following are considered as the general features in neurocomputing model[7].

Each processing element typically has its own small local memory, which stores the values of some previously computed results along with the weighting coefficients which are usually modifiable through learning based on some learning rules. The processing that each element does is determined by a transfer function which is a mathematics formula that decides the output of an element from the sum of all the weighted inputs connecting from the preceding processing elements. A neural network is formed by connecting these processing elements into layers divided into groups having some common connecting patterns.

It was found that the processing speed of an actual physical neuron is in the order of few millisecond that is slow as compared with the conventional high speed computer clocking in the order of nanosecond. However human brain can process a very complicated image in the order of a second, implying that the number of processing steps in the actual neural network is around 100 steps[8]. Neurocomputing is inherent with massively parallel distributed processing to realise the 100 steps of neurocomputation. Inputs from the external or previous processing elements are, after a simple threshold processing, fanout to the succeeding processing elements. Each processing element independently receives inputs from many other processing elements and compute output which is again distributed to many other succeeding processing elements, realizing the massively parallel computing network.

Such a massively parallel computing is often mathematically modelled as a kind of matrix multiplication. Thus the weighted inputs from a group of processing elements(neurons) in one layer are connected to a group of processing elements(neurons) in another layer such that,

$$B[i] = \sum_{j=1}^{N} w_{i,j} A[j]$$

where $B[i]$ is weighted sum input of a processing element in the next layer, and $w_{i,j}$ are called the weights which multiply to outputs of the processing elements $A[j]$ in the preceding layer.

Since the connections are only from some processing elements in one layer to a processing element in another layer, the weight matrix $w_{i,j}$ is usually a very sparse matrix so that the above expression may be rewritten as,

$$B[i] = \sum_{n=1}^{N} (w_i)_n A[J(n)]$$

where N is the number of input connection to the $i\text{-}th$ processing element(neuron) and $J(n)$ is the list of indirect addresses. $((w_i)_n)$ and $J(n)$ can be easily aligned into vectors in the memory, so as to utilize vector facilities in comtemporary supercomputers(vector machines). The indirect addressing in $A[J(n)]$, however is a time consuming operation for vector and connection machine[9].

In machines with pipelined main memory as in the CPC, indirect addressing can be made without extra time because there is no memory access conflict.

Indirect addressing takes place in a number of problems involving sparse matrices. Finite element methods for three dimensional structures is a typical example of such a problem. Indirect addressing is also needed in algorithms such as FFT(Fast Fourier Transformation) which is a computing technique essential in the voice and image processing.

After decades of work in voice and image recognition using the algorithm approach in the conventional computer, we are still not reaching the level of competency of an infant for voice and image recognition. Neurocomputings modelling the neural operations in the brain essentially aim for tackling such a challenge. However the raw input from some sensing devices can not directly be processed by the neural networks. A conversion or transformation preprocessing such as FFT is frequently used.

Let the combination of 'two vector accesses + one direction access + one floating point multiplication + one floating point add ' be called a 'NOP', standing for an unit 'Neuron Operation' (not standing for Non effective Operation !). 'NOP' would also be a reasonable measure for finite element calculations and FFT. One NOP can be made equivalent to two FLOPS in CPC, and 10 GNOPS (10 Giga Neuron Operations Per Second) would be achieved in QFP CPC. In vector and connection machine however a NOP would need about 10 FLOPS time so that 1 GFLOPS machine would only run at the speed of 100MNOPS.

Based on the 10GNOPS in CPC if we assume that the number of processing units in a neural network to be 10^7 and the number of synaptical connections(weights) per processing element to be 10^3 then the response time of one second is achievable. Such an estimation shows that it is still three order below the number of actual neurons in our brain which is in the order of 10 billion. Also traditional estimation on number of synaptical connections is in the order of thousand to ten thousand, thus our estimation is based on the lower end of the number of synaptical connections. However as compared with the current neural network simulation done with few thousands of processing elements(neurons) with less than thousand sypnatical connections per processing element, this is considered as three to four order of improvement.

A novel computational schema on assigning a certain size of information represented as numeral, symbol or both within a logic unit and a memory unit of a computer is also conceived for the CPC machine. This schema, called BL(base-limit) schema, lets both numeral and symbol be processed simultanously, has never be done before in conventional computer architecture[10,11]. The integration of numeral and symbol computing in CPC by using BL schema shall be useful for knowledge information processing. This view is based on the current trend in knowledge information processing which is grossly divided into the symbolic approach such as rule based or logic based processing, and numeral approach such as neurocomputing which seems to suit well for image or voice processing. Probably they may be integrated for some practical or more profound reasons as there are some studies show that the brain of human being is divided into left and right portion with logical processings being done in the left brain and image processings being done in the right brain.

In conclusion we have illustrated the basic operational principle of **QFP and** some of the potential applications of this technology in the emerging neurocomputing research.

Acknowledgement
K.F.Loe would like to thank T.Soma for beneficial discussion.

References

1. E.Goto, First RIKEN Symp. of Josephson Electronics, pp48-54. Mar 1984.

2. K.F.Loe and E.Goto, IEEE Trans. Magn., vol.MAG-21, pp.884-887, Mar 1985.

3. Y.Harada, H.Nakane, N.Miyamoto, U.kawabe, E.Goto, and T.Soma, IEEE Trans. Magn., vol.MAG-23,NO.5,Sep 1987.

4. K.Shimizu and E.Goto, 2th RIKEN Symposium on Josephson Electronic, pp10-28, Mar 1985. Revised version will appear in IEEE Trans. on Computers.

5. H.Nakane,4th RIKEN Symposium on Josephson Electronics, pp75-77, Mar 1987.

6. Y.Uchikawa and M.Kotani, 4th RIKEN Symposium on Josephson Electronics, pp24-29, Mar 1987.

7. D.E.Rumelhart, J.L.McClelland and PDP Research Group, Parallel Distributed Processing, Pub.MIT Press, 1986.

8. J.A.Feldman, Cognitive Science, 9, pp205-254, 1985.

9. D.Hillis, The Connection Machine, MIT Press, 1985.

10. M.Sato, 4th RIKEN Symposium on Josephson Electronics, pp30-37, Mar 1987.

11. M.Sato, 5th RIKEN Symposium on Josephson Electronics, pp9-16, Mar 1988.

A PROPOSED GENERALIZATION OF THE TOPOLOGY
OF THE CONNECTION MACHINE

M. C. Lee, C. L. Tan and H. H. Teh†

Department of Information Systems & Computer Science

National University of Singapore

Lower Kent Ridge Road

Singapore 0511

Republic of Singapore

Abstract - The choice of a topology is one of the central issues in the design of the interconnection network for the Connection Machine, and for massively parallel machines in general. The binary hypercube, or boolean n-cube, has been a popular choice among designers and is implemented on many parallel machines, including the Connection Machine. This paper proposes a generalization of the traditional binary hypercube using a method of construction based on the product of group graphs. This provides us with a framework whereby we can classify a large class of graphs as hypercube structures. The most general of these is the generalized hypercube (GHC) first proposed by Bhuyan & Agrawal, and the simplest the binary hypercube. We discuss some topological properties of this class of graphs constructed from the product of group graphs and address the problem of message routing in an interconnection network that has such a topology.

---

†   *Institute of Systems Science, National University of Singapore*

1. Introduction

In recent years, a new breed of supercomputers has emerged. This is the class of *massively parallel computers*, one of which may contain thousands, perhaps even millions, of small processors arranged on an interconnection network. Each processor alone is neither powerful nor fast, but the coordinated interaction of all the processors working together on a single problem results in processing speeds that are in the supercomputer range. One of the forerunners of this type of machines is the Connection Machine [Hillis 85]. Current Connection Machine systems consist of either 16,384 or 65,536 1-bit processors, each with 4,096 bits of memory, arranged on a high-speed packet-switched interconnection network with a hypercube topology. Benchmarks on the Connection Machine have obtained results of 2000 MIPS for 32-bit additions and 6000 MIPS for document retrieval in database applications [Waltz 87]. These speeds can be considered to be Cray-class.

The performance of the Connection Machine system depends on a balance between the various system components [Reed & Grunwald 87]. Optimal performance is obtained when there is no single system bottleneck. Thus the interconnection network must be fast enough to support the rate of computation of the processors. The performance of the network then becomes an important factor in determining the overall performance of the Connection Machine system.

The design of the interconnection network for a massively parallel computer system is a complex and difficult technical issue. We want good performance at a low cost. One of the central issues in interconnection network design is the choice of a suitable topology for the network. This is the pattern in which all the processors are hardwired. Ultimately, messages between processors will travel across the physical links between processors; the topology will thus affect the speed in which communication can take place amongst processors. The topology also determines the number of neighbouring processors a particular processor is connected to and thus the number of I/O ports that must be provided on a processor. This affects the overall cost of the network. A good topology therefore minimizes communication delay amongst processors and the number of links in the network. Another problem in interconnection network design is the algorithm for the routing of messages through the network. The routing algorithm must be simple and not result in traffic congestion when the load on the system is heavy. It must also be robust in the face of failures of either processors or links.

The *binary hypercube* (or *boolean n-cube*) has always been a popular choice of topology for interconnection networks. Current Connection Machines are built on a hypercube topology. The n-dimensional binary hypercube consists of 2^n processors labelled from 0 to 2^{n-1}. A link connects two processors if and only if the binary representations of the labels of the two processors differ by exactly one bit. Fig. 1 shows binary hypercubes for the cases when $n = 3$ and 4. The binary hypercube can be visualized as an n-dimensional cube with a processor placed at each corner, with each dimension of the cube having two processors. The advantages of the hypercube are its small diameter, uniformity, existence of many redundant paths between any

174

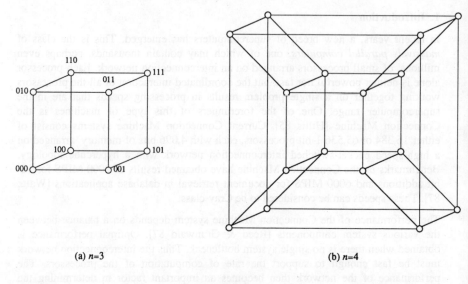

(a) *n*=3   (b) *n*=4

Fig. 1. Binary Hypercubes.

pair of processors and a simple routing algorithm for messages. Also, many other topologies, such as the binary tree, can be embedded in the hypercube [Wu 85], enabling algorithms with communication patterns that match these other topologies to be run on a hypercube topology without any modification. The main disadvantages of the hypercube are the logarithmic increase in the number of links per processor as the size of the network grows and the fact that it can only be increased by a factor of 2.

Bhuyan and Agrawal proposed a *generalized hypercube* (GHC) structure that can support any number of processors and still retain many of the desirable properties of the traditional binary hypercube [Bhuyan & Agrawal 84]. They show that many other topologies, such as the *nearest neighbor mesh* or *torus*, are special cases of the GHC. The GHC is constructed using a *mixed radix number system*. Let N be the number of processors in the network. Express N as a product of r integers denoted by m_i where $1 \leq i \leq r$ and each $m_i > 1$, i.e.

$$N = m_r \times m_{r-1} \times \cdots \times m_2 \times m_1.$$

Each processor X between 0 and $N-1$ can then be labelled as an r-tuple $(x_r x_{r-1} \cdots x_2 x_1)$ with each *coordinate* of the tuple $0 \leq x_i \leq (m_i - 1)$ such that

$$X = \sum_{i=1}^{r} (x_i \times \prod_{j=0}^{i-1} m_j)$$

where $m_0 = 1$. A processor is connected to another if and only if the labels of the two processors in the mixed radix number system differ by one and only one coordinate. In other words, a processor $(x_r x_{r-1} \cdots x_{i+1} x_i x_{i-1} \cdots x_2 x_1)$ will be connected to all processors $(x_r x_{r-1} \cdots x_{i+1} x_i' x_{i-1} \cdots x_2 x_1)$ for all $1 \leq i \leq r$, where x_i' takes all integer values between 0 and $(m_i - 1)$ except x_i itself. Thus the GHC structure consists of r

dimensions with m_i processors along the ith dimension. A processor in an axis is connected to all other processors along the same axis, i.e., it has $(m_i - 1)$ neighbors.

Example 1: Let $N = 24 = 4 \times 3 \times 2$. A processor X can be expressed in the mixed radix number system as a 3-tuple between (000) and (321). The GHC structure defined has 3 dimensions with 2 processors along the first dimension, 3 processors along the second and 4 processors along the third. Fig. 2 shows a diagram of the structure. For the sake of clarity, not all links are shown.

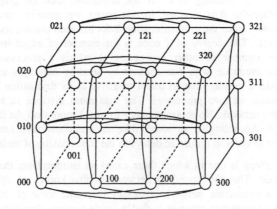

Fig. 2. A 4 * 3 * 2 GHC-structure.

Processor (000) is connected to processor (001) along one dimension, to (010) and (020) along a second dimension and to (100), (200) and (300) along the third dimension.

In this paper, we propose a generalization of the binary hypercube topology of the Connection Machine using a method of construction based on a binary operation on graphs known as the *cartesian product* of graphs. We apply this operation on a class of symmetric graphs known as *group graphs*. This provides us with a general framework in which to construct all structures that can be classified as hypercubes. The most general topology we obtain is the GHC and the simplest the traditional binary hypercube. In between these two cases, we obtain many other topologies that retain the properties of the hypercube. We study some of the topological properties of these graphs and present an algorithm for finding all the shortest paths between any two nodes in a group graph. We then extend this algorithm to find all possible paths between any pair of nodes. Finally, we discuss the problem of message routing in a network with a topology that can be described as a product of group graphs.

2. Preliminaries

In this section, we introduce some concepts and notations in graph theory that will be useful for our subsequent discussion. A network of processors can be naturally modelled as a *graph*, with *nodes* representing processors and *edges* connection links between processors. Certain properties of the network can thus be obtained by analyzing the topological properties of the underlying graph representing the network.

Let G be a graph. The set of nodes of G is denoted by $V(G)$ and the set of edges of G by $E(G)$. An element in $E(G)$ is represented as an ordered pair uv where $u,v \in V(G)$. If the ordering of uv is not important, then the graph is said to be *undirected*; otherwise it is *directed*. In this paper, we concern ourselves with only undirected graphs, since the communication links between processors are always full-duplex channels. The *degree* of a node is the number of edges incident on it and represents the number of other processors to which a processor is connected. Processors communicate with one another by sending messages across links. The number of links a message has to travel to arrive at its destination is known as the *distance* between the two processors. The maximum distance in a network is the *diameter* of the network. No message needs to travel more than the diameter to reach its destination. Accordingly, we would like an interconnection network to have a small diameter in order to minimize delays in the transmission of messages.

A *symmetric* graph is one in which there exists an isomorphism mapping a node to any other node. The corresponding network is also known as symmetric. Every processor in a symmetric network possesses the same view of the network. One advantage of a symmetric network is that a single routing algorithm can be used for every processor. Another advantage is that mathematical analysis of the network is simpler. A symmetric network must necessarily has the same degree for every node. A graph is said to be *k-regular* if every node in the graph has degree k.

The *fault tolerance* of a graph [Akers & Krishnamurthy 84] is defined as the maximum number of nodes that can fail before a graph becomes disconnected. A k-regular graph therefore has a fault tolerance of $k-1$.

We can define many operations on graphs. One of the binary operations is the *cartesian product* [Behzad et al 79] or simply *product* of graphs. The product $G = G_1 \times G_2$ has $V(G) = V(G_1) \times V(G_2)$ and two nodes (u_1, u_2) and (v_1, v_2) of G are connected by an edge if and only if either

$$u_1 = v_1 \text{ and } u_2 v_2 \in E(G_2)$$

or

$$u_2 = v_2 \text{ and } u_1 v_1 \in E(G_1).$$

Fig. 3 shows an example. The product operation is both commutative and associative [Chan 71]. Three other properties of the product operation that will be useful to us in this paper are stated below; the proofs can be found in [Chan 71]:

1. The product of two symmetric graphs is also symmetric.

2. If $u \in G_1$ has degree k_1 and $v \in G_2$ has degree k_2, then $(u,v) \in G_1 \times G_2$ has degree $k_1 + k_2$.

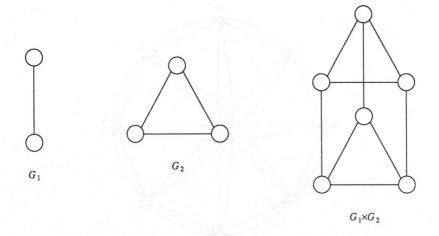

Fig. 3. Product of graphs.

3. If G_1 and G_2 have diameters d_1 and d_2 respectively, then $G_1 \times G_2$ has diameter $d_1 + d_2$.

A class of symmetric graphs that are of interest to us are the *group graphs* [Teh & Shee 76]. Group graphs have been proposed as a source of interconnection network topologies [Akers & Krishnamurthy 84]. A group graph is constructed as follows: Let $<H,+>$ be a group and $A \subseteq H$. Then the group graph, G, generated by A in $<H,+>$ has $V(G) = H$ and

$$E(G) = \{uv \mid u,v \in H \text{ and } u^{-1} + v \in A\}$$

where u^{-1} is the inverse of u in $<H,+>$. Informally, G is the graph which has H as its set of nodes and which has a directed edge drawn from a node u to all nodes obtained by adding u to every element in A. Here, we refer to the group operation $+$ as adding. A group graph constructed from this definition is directed, but we will show by the next example how we can obtain an undirected graph in the same manner. The group $<H,+>$ can be any group and the generator set A any subset of H.

Example 2: Consider the group $<Z_8,+_8>$, where $Z_8 = \{0,1,2,3,4,5,6,7\}$ and $+_8$ denotes the *addition modulo 8* operation. Let the generator set be $\{1,4,7\}$. The group graph generated is shown in fig. 4.

Notice that edges between two nodes occur in pairs, with one going in one direction and the other in the opposite direction. We can thus replace the two directed edges by a single undirected edge. In general, if the generator set A contains elements and their inverses in $<H,+>$, then if there is an edge from u to v, there will also be an edge in the opposite direction, i.e. from v to u. Such a directed graph can be converted into an undirected graph by replacing the two directed edges between a pair of nodes by a single undirected edge.

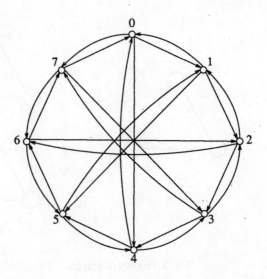

Fig. 4. Group graph.

Group graphs are always symmetric [Teh & Shee 76]. The degree of a node in a group graph is k, i.e. it is k-regular, where k is the number of elements in the generator set A. Consequently, the fault tolerance of a group graph is $k-1$. The number of edges in a group graph is $\dfrac{n \times k}{2}$ where n is the number of nodes in the graph (or, equivalently, the number of elements in H). Many of the common graphs can be generated by groups. For example, the complete graph, the ring (or cycle) and the 1-dimensional hypercube are all generated by the basic group $<Z_n,+_n>$, with different generator sets. The complete graph of size n is generated by $A = \{1,2,3,...,n-1\}$ in $<Z_n,+_n>$ while the ring of n nodes is generated by $A = \{1,n-1\}$ in the same group. The 1-dimensional hypercube (or the simple path of length 1) is generated by $A = \{1\}$ in $<Z_2,+_2>$. These three graphs are shown in fig. 5 where two edges going in opposite directions are replaced by a single edge with two arrow heads. The more complicated graphs, like the GHC, can be constructed by the product of group graphs. The next section describes how this can be done.

3. Hypercubes and GHCs as products of group graphs

An n-dimensional hypercube can be constructed by the product of group graphs in a recursive way. The boolean n-cube K_n is defined as $K_{n-1} \times K_1$ [Behzad et al 79]. K_1 is simply the 1-dimensional hypercube. In other words, the boolean n-cube is obtained by taking the product of K_1 with itself n times. Fig. 6 shows the derivation of K_4. The operation $K_{n-1} \times K_1$ is in fact equivalent to taking two $(n-1)$-dimensional hypercubes and joining the corresponding nodes with edges to obtain an n-

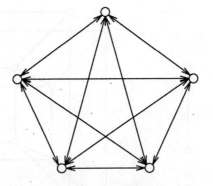

(a) Complete graph of size 5.

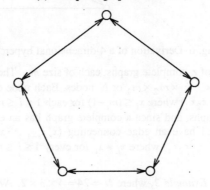

(b) Ring of 5 nodes

(c) 1-dimensional hypercube

Fig. 5. Three common group graphs.

dimensional hypercube [Saad & Schultz 85].

The GHC can also be constructed using the product of group graphs. As before we let

$$N = m_r \times m_{r-1} \times \cdots \times m_2 \times m_1.$$

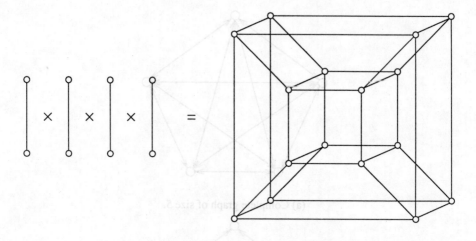

Fig. 6. Derivation of a 4-dimensional hypercube.

We take the products of r complete graphs, each of size m_i. The graph we obtain as a result has $m_r \times m_{r-1} \times \cdots \times m_2 \times m_1$ or N nodes. Each node can be represented by an r-tuple $(x_r x_{r-1} \cdots x_2 x_1)$ where $x_i \leq (m_i - 1)$ for each $1 \leq i \leq r$. From the discussion on the products of graphs, and since a complete graph has an edge connecting every pair of nodes, we will have an edge connecting $(x_r x_{r-1} \cdots x_{i+1} x_i x_{i-1} \cdots x_2 x_1)$ to $(x_r x_{r-1} \cdots x_{i+1} x_i' x_{i-1} \cdots x_2 x_1)$ where $x_i \neq x_i'$ for every $1 \leq i \leq r$. The resulting graph is therefore a GHC.

Example 3: Consider *Example 2*, where $N = 24 = 4 \times 3 \times 2$. We take the product of the complete graphs of sizes 4, 3 and 2 respectively, and the result is as shown in fig. 7.

This method of construction of the GHC and the binary hypercube using the product of group graphs provides us with a general framework for classifying a particular topology as a hypercube structure. All hypercube stuctures can be expressed as a product of group graphs. The simplest of these is the boolean n-cube obtained by the product of K_1 which is the simplest non-trivial graph, and the most general the GHC obtained by the product of complete graphs which are essentially the "largest" graphs for any given number of nodes. In between, we have a host of possibilities produced by the products of group graphs other than the complete graph and K_1 - hypercube structures which are more general than the boolean n-cube but more restricted than the GHC. These restricted forms of GHC include the torus, the cube-connected cycles and many other topologies. The next section will examine the topological properties of these restricted GHCs produced by the products of group graphs.

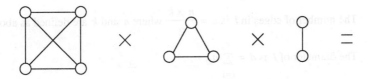

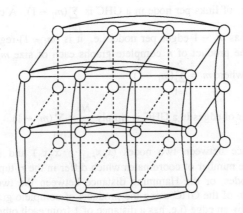

Fig. 7. Product of complete graphs of sizes 4, 3 and 2.

4. Topological properties of products of group graphs

Suppose we have r groups $(H_1,*_1), (H_2,*_2),...,(H_r,*_r)$ of size $n_1, n_2, ..., n_r$ respectively. For each group $(H_i,*_i)$, we choose a generator set $A_i \subseteq H_i$ with k_i elements. Assume that each generator set A_i contains elements and their inverses in $(H_i,*_i)$. Then A_i will generate an undirected group graph G_i in $(H_i,*_i)$. From the properties of group graphs, G_i has n_i nodes and $\dfrac{n_i \times k_i}{2}$ edges. G_i is also k_i-regular. Let the diameter of G_i be d_i. We can construct a restricted GHC I by taking the product of all the group graphs G_i, i.e.

$$I = G_r \times G_{r-1} \times \cdots \times G_1.$$

We list some properties of the graph I:

1. I is symmetric with $n = \displaystyle\prod_{i=1}^{r} n_i$ nodes.

2. I is k-regular where $k = \displaystyle\sum_{i=1}^{r} k_i$ and therefore has a fault tolerance of $k-1$.

3. The number of edges in I is $e = \dfrac{n \times k}{2}$ where n and k are defined as above.

4. The diameter of I is $d = \sum_{i=1}^{r} d_i$.

By making use of the above results, the following observations made for GHCs in [Bhuyan & Agrawal 84] follows immediately:

1. The number of links per node in a GHC is $\sum_{i=1}^{r} (m_i - 1)$. A complete graph with m_i nodes has $m_i - 1$ edges per node, i.e. it is $(m_i - 1)$-regular. Thus a GHC, which is the product of r complete graphs each of size m_i, $1 \leq i \leq r$, will be m-regular where $m = \sum_{i=1}^{r} (m_i - 1)$.

2. The number of edges in a GHC is simply $\dfrac{N}{2} \times \sum_{i=1}^{r} (m_i - 1)$.

3. The distance between two nodes $(x_r x_{r-1} \cdots x_2 x_1)$ and $(y_r y_{r-1} \cdots y_2 y_1)$ is equal to the number of coordinates which differ in the r-tuple representation of the two nodes, or the Hamming distance between the two nodes. From the construction of the GHC using the products of complete graphs, two nodes are connected by an edge (i.e. has a distance of 1 from each other) if and only if the r-tuple representation of the two nodes differ by exactly one coordinate; thus two processors will be seperated by at least the distance equal to the number of different coordinates in the r-tuples representing the two processors, or the Hamming distance between the two processors.

4. Since the diameter for any complete graph is 1, the diameter of a GHC is r.

As illustrated in this section, we can study the topological properties of restricted GHCs produced by the product of group graphs using graph theoretic techniques. This simplify the analysis of these structures. In the next three sections, we address the problem of routing of messages in a network with a restricted GHC topology.

5. Shortest paths in a group graph

Let G be a group graph generated in a group $<H,+>$ by a set $A = \{a_k, a_{k-1}, \ldots, a_2, a_1\}$. We want to find all the shortest paths from a source node s to every node in G. Once we know this, we can apply the necessary transformation to determine all the possible shortest paths between any pair of nodes in G:

We define a *shortest path tree* T from s in G as follows:

1. s is the root of T and has subtrees which are themselves shortest path trees with roots corresponding to those nodes that are a distance of 1 from s; and

2. if a node v in T is at a distance of h from s, then v cannot appear again in T at a distance greater than h from s.

For a group graph, it is relatively easy to construct the shortest path tree. We know that by adding s to $a_i \in A$ for $1 \le i \le k$, we will obtain those nodes that are a distance of 1 from s. We then repeat this step for all the nodes we have obtained and check that we do not include those nodes that have already appeared at a level higher up in the shortest path tree.

Example 4: Consider the group graph in fig. 4. Let 0 be the source node. The shortest path tree T is constructed as shown in fig. 8.

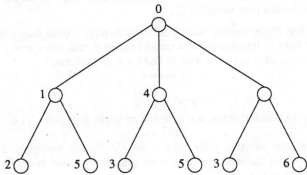

Fig. 8. A shortest path tree.

After the shortest path tree T has been obtained, we perform a preorder traversal of T and note the distance of each node from s. We store the preorder traversal of the nodes in a list L and the corresponding distance in another list D. An algorithm to retrieve all shortest paths from s to a node v is as follows:

1. Scan L sequentially for an occurence of v. Suppose $L[k]=v$. Then v has a shortest distance of $D[k]$ from s.

2. Scanning D backwards from k, we retrieve the nodes corresponding to the first occurence of $D[k]-1, D[k]-2, \cdots, 1$, say $w_{k-1}, w_{k-2}, \cdots, w_1$ respectively. Then the path $sw_1w_2 \cdots w_{k-2}w_{k-1}v$ is a shortest path from s to v with a distance of $D[k]$.

3. Continue scanning L forward from k, look for the next occurence of v. If found, repeat step 2; else if the end of L is reached, stop.

4. Repeat step 3.

Example 5: Consider the shortest path tree in *Example 4*. The lists L and D are shown below:

L	0	1	2	5	4	3	5	7	3	6
D	0	1	2	2	1	2	2	1	2	2

To find all the shortest paths from 0 to 5, we scan L for 5's and obtain the distance 2. Then we scan the list D for the first occurence of 1 and obtain nodes 1. Hence a shortest path from 0 to 5 is along 0-1-5 of length 2. Continuing with the algorithm, we obtain another shortest path along 0-4-5.

If we want to find all the shortest paths from a source node u other than s to a node v in G, we will have to first determine a transformation f that maps u to s involving only the group operation +, i.e. we want to find a $c \in H$ such that
$$f(u) = s$$
where
$$f(x) = x + c.$$
We then apply the transformation to v to obtain an image node, say v', i.e.
$$f(v) = v'$$
and retrieve all the shortest paths from s to v'. Finally we apply the inverse transformation f^{-1} to the nodes on the shortest paths from s to v' to obtain the actual shortest paths from u to v.

6. All possible paths in a group graph

We can use the shortest path algorithm to find all possible paths between any two nodes in a group graph G by applying it to a *path tree* instead of a shortest path tree. A path tree T from a source node s in G is defined in the following way:

1. T has root s and subtrees which are also path trees with roots corresponding to those nodes that are at a distance of 1 from s; and

2. a node v can only appear exactly once along a path from the root s. In other words, v cannot be an ancestor of itself in T .

The second condition in the definition of a path tree traces all possible paths from s while avoiding cycles.

After we have obtained the path tree T', we construct the lists L' and D' by an inorder traversal as before. The application of the shortest path algorithm to the list L' and D' will retrieve all possible paths from s to a node v. For any other source node besides s, we perform the necessary transformation as described in the last section.

7. Message routing in a restricted GHC

In an interconnection network I whose topology can be described by the product of r group graphs $G_r, G_{r-1}, ..., G_1$, a processor can be represented by an r-tuple

$(x_r x_{r-1} \cdots x_{2_1})$. Each coordinate x_i then corresponds to a particular node in a group graph G_i. The r-tuple representation of a processor therefore specifies which particular nodes the processor correspnds to in the various group graphs, which are the constituents of the product operation. To route messages between two processors $(x_r x_{r-1} \cdots x_2 x_1)$ and $(y_r y_{r-1} \cdots y_2 y_1)$, we make use of the same technique used in hypercubes and GHCs: equalize those coordinates which are different in the two r-tuples, one by one. In other words, in each cycle, we pass the message to a processor which has one more coordinate that is identical to the destination processor.

Example 6: Suppose we want to route a message between two processors $(p_r p_{r-1} \cdots p_2 p_1)$ and $(q_r q_{r-1} \cdots q_2 q_1)$ in I. We can pass the message along
$(p_r p_{r-1} \cdots p_2 p_1) \rightarrow (q_r p_{r-1} \cdots p_2 p_1) \rightarrow (q_r q_{r-1} \cdots p_2 p_1) \rightarrow \cdots \rightarrow$
$(q_r q_{r-1} \cdots q_2 p_1) \rightarrow (q_r q_{r-1} \cdots q_2 q_1)$
with one coordinate being equalized in one cycle.

Note that in general, in one cycle, a message may pass through more than one link. That is to say when we pass a message to the processor that has one more coordinate that is identical to the destination processor, we may have to perform routing too. This is not necessary in the boolean n-cube nor the GHC because two processors with exactly one differing coordinate always have a link connecting them. This routing problem is solved when we observe that, by the definition of the product of graphs, processors with only one different coordinate in their r-tuple representation, say in position i, correspond to nodes in the same group graph, G_i. Therefore we can apply the shortest path algorithm described in section 5 to perform the required routing in each cycle.

Example 7: Consider the first cycle in *Example 6* when we have to route the message from $(p_r p_{r-1} \cdots p_2 p_1)$ to $(q_r p_{r-1} \cdots p_2 p_1)$. The problem becomes one of finding the shortest path from p_r to q_r in G_r. Suppose by applying the shortest path algorithm, we obtain a shortest path $p_r p_{r_1} p_{r_2} p_{r_3} q_r$ of length 4. Then we can route the message along
$(p_r p_{r-1} \cdots p_2 p_1) \rightarrow (p_{r_1} p_{r-1} \cdots p_2 p_1) \rightarrow (p_{r_2} p_{r-1} \cdots p_2 p_1) \rightarrow (p_{r_3} p_{r-1} \cdots p_2 p_1) \rightarrow$
$(q_r p_{r-1} \cdots p_2 p_1)$.

For a single group graph G_i we need the vectors L_i and D_i to find a shortest path between any two nodes. For the entire interconnection network I composed of r group graphs, we need to store r vectors of L and D in each processor in order to perform routing in any of the group graphs. If r and the sizes of all the group graphs are small, then the extra storage we require is not much.

We can route messages in the individual group graphs by finding a possible path between two processors instead of the shortest path. This may lead to an increase in the time delay in communication because any path must be equal to or longer than the shortest path between two processors. However, this must be done when all shortest paths between two processors become unavailable, which may happen when either processor or link fails. Hence we can keep two sets of vectors in each processor, one for the shortest paths and one for all possible paths. In normal circumstances, we use the vectors for the shortest paths to perform routing of messages. When all shortest paths become unavailable due to any fault in the network, we can use the vectors for all the possible paths to route messages. In this way, the robustness of the routing algorithm is greatly increased.

8. Conclusion

In this paper, we have proposed a generalization of the hypercube topology by providing a general framework for classifying a large class of graphs as general hypercube structures. This framework is based on the product of group graphs. We show how the traditional hypercube - the boolean n-cube - and the GHC, can be expressed as the product of the simple path of length 1 and complete graphs respectively. In general, we can use any group graph for the product operation. In this way, we will obtain a topological structure that retains many of the properties of the traditional hypercube but is able to support any number of processors as opposed to the 2^n processors requirement of the boolean n-cube. We then list certain topological properties of products of group graphs and study the problem of routing in an interconnection network with such a topology.

We have only touched on the surface of a rich source of hypercube-like topological structures that may be useful for implementation on the interconnection networks of massively parallel machines, particularly the Connection Machine. Further work can be done on the use of graph theoretic techniques in the study of the topological properties and performance of these graphs. Another area of research is to study how other topologies can be embedded in this class of hypercube structures. This will give an idea of the types of applications that are suitable for execution on these topologies. The result of all this research may reveal certain optimal interconnection strategies that may improve drastically the performance of massively parallel machines.

References

[Akers & Krishnamurthy 84] S. B. Akers & B. Krishnamurthy, "Group Graphs as Interconnection Networks," *Dig. Papers, 14th Annual Symp. Fault Tolerant Computing*, pp 422-427, June 1984.

[Behzad et al 79] M. Behzad, G. Chartland & L. Lesniak-Foster, *Graphs & Digraphs*, Wadsworth Internation Group, 1979.

[Bhuyan & Agrawal 84] L. N. Bhuyan & D. P. Agrawal, "Generalized Hypercube and Hyperbus Structures for a Computer Network," *IEEE Trans on Comp*, Vol C-33, No 4, April 1984.

[Chan 73] Y. Chan, *Graph Design*, MSc Thesis, Nanyang University, Singapore, 1973.

[Hillis 85] D. Hillis, *The Connection Machine*, MIT Press, Cambridge, Mass., 1985.

[Reed & Grunwald 87] D. A. Reed & D. C. Grunwald, "The Performance of Multicomputer Interconnection Networks," *Computer*, Vol 20, No 6, June 1987.

[Saad & Schultz 85] Y. Saad & M. H. Schultz, "Topological Properties of Hypercubes," *Yale University Research Report YALEU/DCS/RR-389*, June 1985.

[Teh & Shee 76] H. H. Teh & S. C. Shee, *Algebraic Theory of Graphs*, Lee Kong Chian Institute of Mathematics & Computer Science, 1976.

[Waltz 87] D. L. Waltz, "Applications of the Connection Machine," *Computer*, Vol 20, No 1, Jan 1987.

[Wu 85] A. Y. Wu, "Embedding of Tree Networks into Hypercubes," *Journal of Parallel and Distributed Processing*, 2, pp 238-245, 1985.

Preliminary Study of the CPU Performance of the TITAN Compared with that of the CRAY X-MP/1

Erika Misaki
Kok-Meng Lue
Raul H. Mendez
Institute for Supercomputing Research, Recruit Co. Ltd.,
Tokyo, Japan

Abstract

A preliminary performance study of the Ardent TITAN II system is presented. The CPU processing capability is studied by means of a set of benchmark codes which includes the Livermore FORTRAN kernels, the Los Alamos benchmark set and a set of CFD application codes used to evaluate supercomputer performance in earlier studies.

1. INTRODUCTION

Through the emergence of supercomputers numerical simulation has become a powerful new tool for scientists and engineers. The experimental method with its theory-experiment duality has been broadened and enhanced by the introduction of numerical simulation. It is now possible to carry out numerical experiments in cases where experiments are impractical or too expensive to be implemented. From oil recovery to the design of new proteins, numerical simulation has opened untapped areas to science.

Numerical simulation, a process in which the equations of motion describing the physical system (or physical phenomenon) are solved, is today effectively complemented by graphics visualization. Because of the tremendous processing power of supercomputers, scientists and engineers are studying images rather than numerical data. One image in color can summarize megabytes of data facilitating the analysis of results yielded by numerical simulation. Frequently thousands of such images are used in animations which simulate the evolution of physical phenomena. Up to now the transformation of numerical data into images has been done off-line. One of the major bottlenecks has been the limited bandwidth of networking devices and the lack of computational power of display stations. Furthermore, trivial errors, for example in parameter setting, are caught only after visualizing the data on a workstation; causing the entire run to be discarded at considerable cost.

In the Fall of 1985, with advent of the Alliant FX-8 and the Convex C-1, minisupercomputers were introduced in the computer arena. These machines offer cost-performance ratios better than those of supercomputers are now becoming popular. Minisupercomputers became possible after the introduction of CMOS VLSI, enabling them to be air cooled, consume little power and run under UNIX-like operating systems. These systems, currently used as departmental supercomputers, represent an important step in the road towards distributed processing.

This year an equally important step has been taken with introduction of a systems known variously as graphics supercomputers or single-user supercomputers. These new systems attempt to incorporates the vector processing capabilities of minisupercomputers with the 3-d graphics capabilities of superworkstations, allowing in principle direct visualization of the simulations as the calculation proceeds, thus eliminating the networking bottleneck and the the lack of computing power in the graphics displays. These new systems rely on their floating point engines to compute geometrical transformations for their graphics displays. Their ability to interact directly with the model through images as the simulation is being computed will have a profound effect on both science and engineering. Among the new systems are the Stellar GS1000, Ardent Titan and Apollo Domain10000 series.

In this article we compare the performance of the Ardent Kubota Titan system with that of the Cray X-MP/1, describing briefly along the way the architecture and main features of the Titan. The results we report on this benchmark study are preliminary CPU tests. No effort has been made to measure the graphics performance of this system (a component just as important as the CPU processing power in these machines). A more detailed study of the CPU/graphics duality will be published at a later time.

Our tests were run on a Titan2 under the Beta2 release software. Despite the preliminary nature of the software, our tests allow us to surmise the power of the vector processor of the Titan system. A later study based on real applications will permit a more detailed study of the system which will include software features such as the vectorizing and parallelizing compiler.

2. ARCHITECTURE AND TECHNOLOGY OF THE TITAN

The TITAN is a shared memory multiprocessor system consisting up to 4 processors each running at 62.5 nanoseconds clock cycle (16 Mhertz). The processors and the graphics subsystem communicate and access memory (interleaved in 16 banks) through a 256 Megabyte bus.

Like the Cray systems the Titan is a register to register machine. Operands are fetched from memory to vector registers and then routed to functional units for execution. There are 3 functional units: floating point add, multiply and logic, in contrast to the 12 functional units on the Cray X-MP/1. Floating point arithmetic is carried to 64-bit precision. A fetch from memory to vector registers takes 7 clock cycles. Interleaving and a memory cycle of five clocks allow a memory bandwidth of 2 words per cycle, which is also the bandwidth of the bus.

The maximum memory capacity is 128 Mbytes, consisting of four boards, each with a maximum capacity of 32 Mbytes. Systems containing one memory board are interleaved in 8 banks while systems with two or more memory boards are interleaved in 16 banks.

Each processor consists of an integer processor unit and a vector processor unit. There is no dedicated scalar unit *per se* as in today's minisupercomputers and supercomputers.

The vector unit's floating point hardware is built around the 64-bit add, multiply, and divide Weitek floating point chips with a performance of 8 Mflops for addition as well as multiplication and 1 Mflops for division. Thus, the one processor board has a theoretical peak speed of 16 Mflops. Supporting the floating point hardware are a total of 256 vector registers each holding 32 elements totalling to 64 kbytes.

The vector unit under instructions from the integer unit operates on floating point vectors, integer vectors and floating point scalars. In additional, the vector unit is used to perform matrix-matrix multiplications required in graphic processing. The vector instruction set includes gather/scatter instructions to handle indirect memory accesses. The integer unit, on the other hand, is built around a 32-bit MIPS chip (a microprocessor designed with the RISC concept, with a peak performance of 16 MIPS).

Memory accesses are buffered through an instruction and data cache each with a 16 kbytes capacity . The integer unit issues instructions to the vector unit, and handles other control functions as well as compilation (scalar floating point instructions are executed by the vector unit as vector instructions of length one).

Table 1

Hardware Technology		
	CRAY X-MP1	**TITAN**
LOGIC	16-gate arrays 350 psec	2-30000-gate arrays 3 nsec
MEMORY	NA	64K-bit 25 nsec CMOS
	4K-bit RAMS 25 nsec ECL	1 MBIT 100 nsec CMOS

A key feature of the TITAN system is that it is built on the second generation CMOS VLSI technology. These technology is widely available at significantly better cost to performance over the ECL technology employed by Cray X-MP/1 systems. Unlike supercomputers which employ real memory systems, the Titan employs a virtual memory configuration. The main memory is based on a 1 Mbit 100 nsec C-MOS DRAMS while the vector registers and cache employ the 64 Kbit 25 nsec CMOS static RAMS. Logic is built on gate-arrays holding between 20,000 and 30,000 gates with gate delays of 3 nsecs. From table 1 we see that the Titan employs its memory hierarchy devices with speeds corresponding to those employed on supercomputers at lower levels in their memory hierarchy. For example the 25 nsec rams used on the Titan's vector registers and cache are employed in the Main memory of the Cray X-MP/1.

3. BENCHMARKING CODES AND BENCHMARKING CONDITIONS

We shall attempt to characterize the performance of the Titan system by performance comparison with the Cray X-MP/1 on a collection of codes taken from benchmark sets previously used in earlier vector processor performance evaluations. Our goal in this study is to recognize the salient features in the Titan's performance spectrum. A hierarchy of test programs ranging from a collection of FORTRAN kernels to full application codes is used in this study. We have conducted the benchmark test at three different levels of the hierarchy: (1) Program kernels, usually 10-20 lines of FORTRAN loops, to understand the performance in depth: vectorization, for example, (2) Fragments of codes from elementary matrix operations to stripped-down version of production programs and from simple scalar operations to highly vectorizable codes are used to measure performance range of the system, and (3) Full-application codes to represent more accurate picture of system performance.

The Livermore Fortran Kernels, the Los Alamos benchmark set, and 2 fluid dynamics codes are used as the three levels of hierarchy to ascertain the Titan's performance. These include scalar, vector and concurrent vector performance. It is important to note that all codes used for this test are not tuned or hand coded.

Table 2

Characteristics of Los Alamos benchmark codes				
Code	Vectorization (percent)	Predominant vector length	CRAY X-MP 1 (CFT 1.14) (sec)	CRAY X-MP 1 (CFT 77) (sec)
BMK 1 (scalar)	2	61	43.3	17.0
BMK 14 (vector)	99	100	1.3	1.3
BMK 21a (scalar)	18	35	8.3	4.0
BMK 22 (vector)	98	100	7.7	6.9

Table 3

Characteristics of the CFD codes		
Code	Vectorization (percent)	Predominant vector length
VORTEX	98%	20-500
MHD2D	98%	256

Our benchmark tests were run in dedicated mode on a 64 Mbyte Titan II system, hereafter referred to as the Titan, at Kubota Computer in August 23, 1988. Timings on the Cray X-MP/18 at Recruit in Dojima, Osaka, hereafter refereed as the Cray X-MP/1 were performed in August of 1988. It should be emphasized that our tests are CPU benchmarks. And I/O and operating systems overheads are ignored.

4. PERFORMANCE ON LOS ALAMOS & LIVERMORE KERNELS

4.1. LOS ALAMOS KERNELS

BMK1	: Integer Monte Carlo code (virtually no floating point instructions)
BMK5	: Equation of state
BMK11	: Particle-in-cell codes (gather and scatter type memory accesses)
BMK14	: Matrix operations of order 100
BMK21a	: Monte Carlo photon transport code
BMK22	: Linear equations solver via Gaussian elimination (matrix order is 100)

4.2. LIVERMORE FORTRAN KERNELS

LFK1	: Hydro fragment
LFK2	: Incomplete Cholesky-conjugate gradient
LFK3	: Inner product
LFK4	: Banded linear equations
LFK5	: Tri-diagonal elimination (below diagonal)
LFK6	: General linear recurrence equations
LFK7	: Equation of state fragment

LFK8	: ADI integration
LFK9	: Integrate predictors
LFK10	: Difference predictors
LFK11	: First sum
LFK12	: First difference
LFK13	: 2-D particle in cell
LFK14	: 1-D particle in cell
LFK15	: Ordering of scalar operations
LFK16	: Monte Carlo search loop
LFK 17	: Implicit, conditional computation
LFK 18	: 2-D explicit hydrodynamics fragment
LFK 19	: General linear recurrence equation
LFK 20	: Discrete ordinates transport
LFK 21	: Matrix-matrix product
LFK 22	: Planckian distribution
LFK 23	: 2-D implicit hydrodynamics fragment
LFK 24	: Find location of first minimum in array

4.3. SCALAR PERFORMANCE

Because a scalar unit is not incorporated in the Titan, scalar instructions are executed in the vector unit as vectors of unit length.

For scalar applications that are integer arithmetic intensive the Titan can perform surprisingly well. BKM1 of the Los Alamos sets of codes is one such code. As shown in table 4 the Titan 1 at 96.2 sec compares well with 43.3 sec for the Cray X-MP/1 (CFT1.14) being only 2.2 times slower. Such good performance is due to the fact that Titan processes the integers via its Integer Unit in 32-bits chunks as opposed to the 24-bit arithmetic of the Cray.

Table 4

Time required for Los Alamos Kernels (seconds)				
Code	TITAN (BETA 2)		CRAY X-MP 1 (CFT 1.14)	
	Scalar	Vector	Scalar	Vector
BMK 1	96.2	135.2	43.3	NA.
BMK 14	92.7	9.6	NA	1.3
BMK 21a	67.4	63.8	8.3	NA
BMK 22	373.1	59.7	NA	7.7

On the other hand we find that on BMK21a which is nearly all floating point calculation the Cray X-MP/1 (CFT1.14) is 8.1 times faster than the Titan (67.4 sec vs 8.3sec).

Additional insight on the scalar capabilities of the Titan can be obtained from the Livermore loops. Table 5 summarizes the Mflops rates for the six LFK which are not vectorized by both systems. It is interesting to note that across these six loops the performance of either system varies by roughly a factor of 2 (the performance of the Titan varies between 0.9 and 2 Mflops). Additionally, the X-MP/1 is at best 8.9 times faster than the Titan (on LFK17, a fairly complex kernel). On the other hand the Titan approaches the performance of the X-MP/1 within a factor of 3.1 on LFK5, a first order recursion (in fact, out of the nonvectorized six kernels the Titan and the X-MP/1 under CFT77 yield their best performance on this kernel).

Table 5

Scalar LFK loops that are unvectorized across the two systems. (Rates are in MFLOPS; loop lengths are in parentheses.)						
	5(1001)	11(1001)	16(75)	17(101)	19(101)	20(1000)
CRAY X-MP 1 (CFT1.15)1986	6.2	8.3	3.6	11.6	7.6	12.3
(CFT 77) 1986	14.4	12.7	6.2	10.2	13.4	13.2
TITAN (BETA2)	2.0	1.4	0.9	1.3	1.8	1.6

It is noteworthy that both systems reach the lowest performance, among the six loops, 0.9 Mflops and 3.6 Mflops on LFK16 a loop with 10 branches out of 17 statements.

Table 6

Statistics on the six unvectorized LFK by the two systems. (Rates are in MFLOPS)					
	Min	Max	Average	Geometric mean	Harmonic mean
CRAY X-MP 1 (CFT 1.15)1986	3.6	11.6	8.3	7.7	7.0
(CFT 77) 1986	6.2	14.4	11.7	11.3	10.8
TITAN (BETA 2)	0.9	2.0	1.5	1.5	1.4

The range, harmonic mean, and of other statistics summarizing the performance of the six kernels not vectorized by the Titan are shown in Table 6. Notice that the average, geometric and harmonic mean cluster around 1.4 Mflops suggesting that this is representative of the scalar speed of the Titan for the kind of workloads characterized by these kernels (Similarly, the same three parameters for the X-MP/1 are centered about 7.6 Mflops).

4.4. VECTOR PERFORMANCE

On the Los Alamos Kernels we first consider BMK14, a highly vectorizable, basic matrix operation code. In this instance the Titan1 runs 7.4 times slower than the X-MP/1 under CFT1.14 (9.6 sec vs 1.3 sec).

Considering next BMK22 a linear equation solver by Gaussian Elimination for a system of order 100. In this case the Titan1 performance is 7.8 times slower than that of the X-MP/1 under CFT1.14 (59.7 sec vs 7.7 sec). It is noteworthy that this performance is consistent with that of the measurements obtained by Dongarra on his LINPACK benchmark (Gaussian elimination on a linear system of order 100). According to data released by the Argonne National Lab, May 23 1988 the X-MP/1 (CFT77, 8.5 nsec clock) is clocked at 59 Mflops, with the Titan1 at 6.1 Mflops being 9.6

times slower (the difference in speed up being explained by the faster clock as well as the faster compiler).

It is interesting to examine the computing rate versus the memory throughput required by the SAXPY operation in the LINPACK benchmark. If for example SAXPY's execution rate is to be sustained at say 10 Mflops by flowing operands continuously to and from memory, a memory throughput rate of 120 Mbytes/sec, well within the bus bandwidth, is required (the two floating point operations in SAXPY require three operands or 24 Mbytes).

From table 4 we see that the Titan performance on BMK14 and BMK22 yields scalar-vector acceleration ratios, respectively 9.7 and 6.2, well in agreement with the highly vector nature of these two codes.

Table 7 lists the vector performance on the fourteen LFK codes vectorized by both systems: the average vector length is 471. We see on Table 7 that both systems achieve their peak on LFK7, 171 Mflops and 12.2 Mflops respectively. The very high ratio between floating point work and contiguous memory accesses on this kernel accounts for these high rates. Both systems achieved 80% of their respective theoretical peak rates.

Table 7

LFK loops that are vectorized on both machines. (Rates are in MFLOPS, loop lengths in parentheses)			
LFK	**CRAY X-MP/1** (CFT 1.15)	**TITAN** (BETA 2)	
		Vector	*Parallel*
1(1001)	152.3	9.3	17.3
2(101)	27.5	4.0	2.0
3(1001)	135.3	7.4	6.9
4(1001)	42.0	6.2	5.5
6(64)	11.8	2.9	2.9
7(995)	171.4	12.2	19.5
8(100)	115.4	7.9	13.0
9(101)	144.7	9.5	13.2
10(101)	69.1	3.2	4.0
12(1000)	65.5	5.7	6.8
14(1001)	13.1	1.0	1.3
18(100)	111.7	3.7	6.7
21(25)	73.0	10.4	9.8
22(101)	66.3	0.8	0.9

Titan's worst performance is 0.8 Mflops on LFK22, probably because of slow performance on the exponential functione valuation . This rate is 7% of maximum attainable rate of 12.2 Mflops. On the other hand the X-MP/1's worst performance is 12 Mflops on LFK6 (a general recurrence) or 2% of its attainable maximum.

Both systems do well on LFK9, achieving 9.5 Mflops and 145 Mflops or 78% and 85% of their achieved maxima (similar work to LFK 7).

Both systems, however, do poorly on LFK14 which contains irregular memory references. The systems' rates of 1 Mflops and 13 Mflops on this code amount to 8% of their achieved maxima.

Table 8 summarizes various statistics on the 14 kernels vectorized by the two systems. It is noteworthy that the harmonic mean of this sample of Titan vector timings is within a factor of 10 that of the X-MP/1.

Table 8

Statistics on the 14 vectorized LFK by the two systems. (Rates are in MFLOPS)				
	Min	Max	Average	Harmonic mean
CRAY X-MP 1 (CFT 1.15)1986	12.0	171.0	85.6	43.4
TITAN (BETA 2) Vector	0.8	12.2	6.0	4.4
Parallel	0.9	14.4	7.8	3.5

4.5. PARALLEL PERFORMANCE

The Livermore benchmarks we used above were also run using the parallel option. When enabled, this feature of the system distributes automatically the work between the two processors on the Titan2. For the Los Alamos codes tested, the overhead for parallelization was not compensated by the faster execution time. However data on the Livermore loops indicate that the parallel option can significantly improve performance. For example the Titan's performance on LFK7 increases from 12.2 Mflops to 19.5 Mflops (for a vector length of 995). Similarly on LFK9 the performance increases from 9.5 Mflops to 13.2 Mflops (for a vector length of 101).

5. PERFORMANCE ON CFD CODES

As shown on table 9 the vector-scalar accelerations on these codes are 1.8 and 2.1 respectively, corresponding acceleration ratios on the X-MP are 9.9 and 10.6 (CFT1.15). Despite high vector ratios (table 3) in these codes the Titan's vector performance is mediocre. Analysis reveals that a loop accounting for more than 50% of the work in VORTEX has not been vectorized because the present version of the compiler does not support the vectorization of the branching syntax included in the loop. As can be seen

200

on table 9 the untuned Titan's vector timing on MHD2D are nearly the same
as its scalar timings and the same can be said about the X-MP/1 timings.

Table 9

Time required for CFD codes (seconds)				
	CRAY X-MP 1 (CFT 1.14)		TITAN (BETA 2)	
	Scalar	Vector	Scalar	Vector
VORTEX	138.2	13.9	1803.1	996.4
MHD2D Untuned	18.4	18.8	255.6	119.6
Tuned	18.4	3.7	NA	NA

For the purpose of illustration, on table 9, are listed the X-MP/1's tuned
vector timings on MHD2D (this data is taken from an earlier study on
supercomputer performance). In this case tuning amounts to inserting
compiler directives on the FFT routine that consumes most of the work. As
mentioned above similar tuning for the Titan is beyond the scope of the
present work.

6. SUMMARY OF LFK RESULTS

1) Scalar performance. The Titan's harmonic mean of the six LFK loops
not vectorized on both systems is within a factor of 5 of the corresponding
ratio for the X-MP/1.

2) Vector performance. The Titan's harmonic mean of the fourteen LFK
loops vectorized by both systems is within a factor of 10 of the
corresponding rate for the X-MP/1.

3) Parallel performance. The LFK data is mixed on the merits of
parallelization. The effectiveness of parallelization depends on the vector
length and of the contents of the code.

7. CONCLUSION

The above CPU benchmark results suggest that the Titan is a powerful processor of scalars and vectors. One suggestion derived from the present study is that the Titan's performance spectrum, when scaled in the appropriate units, is quite similar to that the X-MP/1. The present data also suggests the remarkable fact that the scaling, which is application dependent, maybe within one order of magnitude or close to one order of magnitude.

It should be emphasized that the above benchmarks were all CPU tests and that I/O and OS overheads have not been accounted for in the present study. A performance study including these factors may lead to different results.

REFERENCES

LUBECK O., MOORE J., MENDEZ R., "A Benchmark Comparison of Three Supercomputers : Fujitsu VP-200, Hitachi S-810/20 and Cray X-MP/2", *IEEE Computer*, Dec. 1983.

DONGARRA J., MARTIN J., WORLTON J., "Computer Benchmarking : paths and pit falls", *IEEE Spectrum*, vol24, no 7., 1987.

McMAHON F., "The Livermore Fortran Kernels : A Computer Test of the Numerical Performance Range", *Lawrence Livermore National Laboratory report UCRL-53745*, Dec. 1986.

LUBECK O., "Supercomputer Performance : The Theory, Practice and Results", *Los Alamos National Laboratory document LA-11204-MS*, Jan. 1988.

Reading List

Compiled by C K Yuen
Dept of Information System and Computer Science
National University of Singapore

This section lists a number of books and articles covering subjects related to the contents of this proceedings.

Babb, R.G. Programming Parallel Processings, Reading, Mass.: Addison Wesley, 1988.

Communications of the ACM, Special Issue on Computer Architecture, January 1985, New York: Association for Computing Machinery, 1985.

Communications of the ACM, Special Issue on Parallel Algorithms, June 1986, New York: Association for Computing Machinery, 1986.

Computer, Special issue on Multiprocessor Technology, June 1985, Los Alamitos, Calif.: IEEE Computer Society, 1985.

Computer, March 1986 issue, Los Alamitos, Calif.: IEEE Computer Society, 1986.

Computer, March 1987 issue, Los Alamitos, Calif.: IEEE Computer Society, 1987.

Computer, Special issue on Interconnection Networks, June 1987, Los Alamitos, Calif.: IEEE Computer Society, 1987.

Computer, Special issue on Systolic Arrays, July 1987, Los Alamitos, Calif.: IEEE Computer Society, 1987.

Computer, Special issue on Synchronization, Coherence and Ordering of Events in Multiprocessors, February 1988, Los Alamitos, Calif.: IEEE Computer Society, 1988.

Computer, Special issue on Artificial Neural Systems, March 1988, Los Alamitos, Calif.: IEEE Computer Society, 1988.

Frenkel, K.A. Evaluation of Two Massively Parallel Machines, Communications of the ACM, vol. 29, No. 8, pp. 752-778, 1986.

Hillis, W.D. The Connection Machine, Cambridge, Mass.: MIT Press, 1985.

Hwang, K. Advanced Parallel Processing with Supercomputer Architectures, Proceedings of the IEEE, vol. 75, No. 10, pp. 1349-1379, 1987.

204

Hwang, K. and Briggs, F.A. Computer Architecture and Parallel Processing, New York: McGraw-Hill, 1985.

Hwang, K. and DeGroot, D. Parallel Processing for Supercomputing and Artificial Intelligence, New York: McGraw-Hill, 1988.

International Journal of High Speed Computing, Singapore: World Scientific Publishing Co. (periodical)

Joseph, M., Prasad, V.R. and Natarajan, N. Multiprocessor Operation System: Abstraction, Design and Implementation, Englewood Cliffs, N.J.: Prentice-Hall, 1984.

Journal of Parallel and Distributed Computing, Orlando, Florida: Academic Press (periodical).

Karplus, W.J. Multiprocessors and Array Processors, San Diego, Calif.: Society of Computer Simulation, 1987.

Kung, S.Y. VLSI Array Processors, Englewood Cliffs, N.J.: Prentice-Hall, 1987.

Norrie, C. Supercomputers for Superproblems: Architectural Introduction, Computer, vol. 17, No. 3, pp. 62-75, 1984.

Parallel Computing, New York: Elsevier North Holland (periodical).

Stone, H.S. High Performance Computer Architecture, Reading, Mass.: Addison Wesley, 1987.

Wise, M. Prolog Multiprocessors, Sydney, Australia: Prentice-Hall, 1986.

Author Index

Chan S.C.	26
Chong Y.J	21
Goto B	163
Hatano Y	89
Hirai K	93
Hsu L.S	26
Kaneda Y	1, 88
Kuwabata K	3
Lee MC	172
Lim H	10
Loe K.P.	26, 163
Low H B	26
Lue K-M	188
Mendez R	188
Misaki Z	188
Ninomiya I	89
Nodera T	73
Oyanagi Y	17
Phua K H	51
Shimasaki M	93
Tan C L	172
Teh H H	172
Tokioka T	18
Tsuda	93
Uemura Y	141
Yasumura M	109
Yuen C K	1, 203

Author Index

Chan S C	26
Chong Y J	21
Goto E	163
Hatano Y	89
Hirai K	93
Hsu L S	26
Kanada Y	i,88
Kuwahara K	3
Lee MC	172
Lim H	10
Loe K F	26,163
Low H B	26
Lue K-M	188
Mendez R	188
Misaki E	188
Ninomiya I	89
Nodera T	73
Oyanagi Y	17
Phua K H	51
Shimasaki M	93
Tan C L	172
Teh H H	172
Tokioka T	19
Tsuda	93
Uemora Y	iii
Yasumura M	109
Yuen C K	i,203